Hope Ignited

The Broken Road to Healing

Grace Pat

Copyright © 2021 by **Grace Pat**

All rights reserved. No part of this publication may be reproduced, distributed, or transmitted in any form or by any means, without prior written permission.

Unless otherwise noted, all Scripture quotations are taken from the Holy Bible, New International Version®, NIV® Copyright © 1973, 1978, 1984, 2011 by Biblica, Inc.® Used by permission. All rights reserved worldwide.

Scripture quotations marked (NASB) are taken from the New American Standard Bible®, Copyright © 1960, 1971, 1977, 1995, 2020 by The Lockman Foundation. Used by permission. All rights reserved. www.Lockman.org.

Renown Publishing
www.renownpublishing.com

Hope Ignited: The Broken Road to Healing / Grace Pat
ISBN-13: 978-1-952602-42-9

To the first man I ever loved. To my first teacher, who gave me a voice in his classroom. To the magical nights we spent storytelling in your magnificent library. Here is to all the nights you'd walk into my room and see me writing. "You should send that to the publisher!" you would say with a smile in your eyes and conviction in your voice. You spoke this book into existence. To my baba—I love you.

To the arms that loved me so tenderly. To the lips that greeted me with a smile every time she laid eyes on me. To the hands that pointed up to the birds, trees, and flowers, and fixed my attention to creation. To the gentle force in my life that kept many at bay. To my mama—you are a mother to many, but I call you my own. I adore you.

To my best friend—the one who loved me at my darkest. You inspire me. I treasure you, Jacob Pat.

To my boys. Professor Joseph, you challenged me. You made it possible to dream again. My handsome Justice, I will always be your loudest cheerleader, because you have shown me not to give up.

I have not forgotten my spiritual family. You know who you are. I count myself blessed and wealthy because you are in my life. You have walked a journey of tears with me and celebrated my breakthroughs. You have prayed me to victory. I have overcome in him alone as you have huddled around me in love, light, and life. I am eternally grateful to you.

CONTENTS

The Road Less Traveled 3
Of Tender Age 5
Miss Claire 9
Marriage 17
Trauma and Healing 29
Identity and Labels 35
Perseverance 45
Prayer and Miracles 55
Forgiveness 69
Grief 79
Resilience 85
Hope 91
Joy 99
Transformation 111
About the Author 117
Notes 118

AUTHOR'S NOTE

The Road Less Traveled

Leaving behind nights of terror and fear
I rise
Into a daybreak that's wondrously clear
I rise
Bringing the gifts that my ancestors gave,
I am the dream and the hope of the slave
I rise
I rise
I rise.[1]

—**Maya Angelou**

Born Muslim, I long struggled with my identity and everything that came with it. I went on an adventure, an adventure God created, that twisted, turned, and threw me off. He took me to a foreign nation, where I had no family or friends. He then *shook me*—my theology, my faith, my beliefs, and my ways. On this adventure, Jesus introduced himself and his ways to me. At the time, I knew in choosing Jesus that I would lose my parents, family, inheritance, friends, and the country I once called home.

I have been travelling a road of denying self, dying to self. It is lonely, painful, and a struggle. There is an undeniable wrestling between soul and spirit. It brought me to my knees and called me to surrender. It is the broken road to healing.

I consider myself one of the wealthiest people in the world because of the journey God has walked me through. He continues to transform my family, relatives, community, and certainly, my nation. He continues to transform my life. "What is more, I consider everything a loss because of the surpassing worth of knowing Christ Jesus my Lord, for whose sake I have lost all things. I consider them garbage, that I may gain Christ" (Philippians 3:8). With joy, I can truly claim this verse.

And he's not done with me yet!

CHAPTER ONE

Of Tender Age

"Where is Allah?" I asked my parents when I was about four years old.

Baba—I call my father Baba—lifted me onto his lap. "That is a sign of your faith," he said. "Never stop questioning."

My Baba gave me permission always to ask questions. That was not the norm in the environment and culture in which I grew up. Sitting on my father's lap, unsatisfied with his non-answer, I simply asked him again, "Well then, where is he?"

He paused for a moment. "He is everywhere!" he answered with certainty.

For most of my childhood, I wanted to be a martyr. This desire was not related to depression or suicidal ideations. It was a desire to go to Heaven, and to do that—to live forever—I had to die. It was not that I wanted to die for myself; I wanted to die for Allah. To be a martyr was undeniably the most honorable thing a devoted

Muslim could desire.

I was not afraid to die. If ending my worldly life meant beginning my afterlife in Heaven, I was all in.

Every morning at school, before classes started, all of the students would assemble in the courtyard. We did our morning prayers. Then, at the top of our lungs, we chanted slogans that millions of other children across our country were also chanting. Every day for my five years in elementary school, we, little children, raised our fists in the air and chanted slogans against our enemies. We would always sing in unison, our singular voice ringing out across our neighborhood. Then we would march out of the courtyard in single file, stomping on the two flags of our enemies that were on the ground, making our way to classrooms.

How were we to know this was not normal? How were we to know this was not right?

At school, we were taught about Islamic history, jihad, and the Quran, but never topics such as music or art. On religious grounds, music and art were forbidden, just like alcohol and dancing in public.

This was all part and parcel of growing up in a society in which young girls like myself were not allowed to play in the streets of our beautiful neighborhoods. We were not allowed to speak to boys. As a girl, I was labelled a rebel and told that I talked too much and asked too many questions. They did not "get" me. I wanted to go out too much, to see places, to travel. If I had been a boy, people would have considered me articulate, curious, and full of intelligent questions. I would have been seen as a perfect future missionary who should be allowed to travel.

Sometimes I wanted to be a boy. I knew if I was, I would have been treated fairly and given the opportunities I craved.

I grew up not in one war, but multiple wars.

My eyes opened to see bloodshed first, instead of sunny skies and diamonds in the sky. My ears heard sirens. My little hands wiped tears. In the mosque, when the lights went out, I used my sense of smell to search for my mother. I know war. A product of war is hate. Hate was a seed planted in us from a young age. We hated nations that we knew little about. We were never given lessons about other countries, only reasons to hate them. Hate them because they are evil. Hate them because they want to obliterate us.

Most children from my community had never left the country. However, I lived a vastly different life. Part of a powerful family, I was allowed to travel with my parents beyond our borders, so I knew slightly more about foreign cultures than other girls did. Still, it was hard not to hate our enemies because that is what teachers and society drilled into us day in and day out. It was also easy to hate, considering what was happening around me.

At school, independent thinking was not encouraged. We were taught conspiracies that prevented us from seeing countries for who they truly were. No one ever posed the question: What are the reasons for being targeted by the world's superpowers?

As a young girl, I knew that my faith was different from that of other Muslims. I did not agree with everything taught to me in school. I did not receive every message preached to me from the pulpit. Still, there was something I just could not put my finger on. There was something inside troubling me, telling me that I could not make it to Heaven on my faith and works alone.

There was a season in my young adult life when I began to believe that my entire childhood was a lie, which prompted the questions: How do you recover from being brainwashed? How does one replace memories and feelings with right thinking and connect them to truth?

In order to break through, I had to have a personal breakdown. It was spiritual hunger for a quality relationship with my Creator God, an intimacy that would allow me to call him "Daddy," so I could feel that I was enough. I grew more desperate for eternal salvation, even if it would cost me my life. I was willing to die.

There is One who washes your feet and mine, even when we reject him.

There is an Advocate for you when there is an accuser.

There is One who has been through every temptation you and I have been through. No matter the season you are in, choose hope.

CHAPTER TWO

Miss Claire

I believe that every child on the planet should receive unconditional love. It breaks my heart that there are millions of children who, for whatever reason, do not experience this from their parents, guardian, or anyone else.

When you were a child, did you receive love without limits or constraints? Were you loved unselfishly by someone who genuinely wanted you to be happy? Were you loved by someone who did not want anything in return? My hope is that your answer is a resounding *yes* and that now—*right now*—you are passing on that unconditional love to others.

In my childhood, there was one person whose love for me exceeded the love of others. You may be thinking it was my parents. No. Although my Mama and Baba loved me unconditionally, there was someone else.

My family allowed Miss Claire into our family to teach me English. She was a short lady who almost never stopped smiling. She was a humbly proud Canadian ESL (English as a Second Language) teacher. But she was also a missionary—I only figured that out years later. I believe my father knew before I did, but that information was never shared with me, perhaps due to the fact that it would have put Miss Claire in danger.

She had a love for me that was even greater than my mother's or father's love. I would like to believe that her love for me—and for everyone else who crossed paths with her—was the love of Jesus. With the way she carried Jesus in her and into a Muslim country, I am certain she touched the lives of numerous people.

Can you imagine what it must have been like for a Christian woman to live, even temporarily, in a strictly Muslim country in the Middle East? In my home country, men and women are not allowed to mix unless women are fully dressed according to Islamic dress codes. Essentially that means women cannot go outside their homes without being fully covered. At times, a face cover is required. Often in public, there are reminders that Hijab is the law for women, including billboards that state, "Hijab means dignity."

Many people—men especially—believe that if a woman exposes her hair or any other body part in public, she is corrupting society. In this way, some people believe that rape and other crimes are caused by uncovered women, so the government has the right to force women to cover up, all to maintain the security of society.

It is not just about clothes, hair, sexual urges, and crime. Teenage girls cannot pick their own friends, speak to boys, or go to the shopping mall without a guardian.

For decades, women have not been allowed to drive in most Islamic countries. They cannot enter sports stadiums. Women are forbidden from studying certain subjects at school, such as engineering or technology. Nursing or medical school is frowned upon due to long and late-hour shifts.

Miss Claire's job was to teach an eager young girl about the English language. To me, though, she was always much more than just a teacher. She was there to extend grace and share divine love. God sent her to me. Her mission was to reveal the love of the Father and to plant the seeds of life in me.

The basics of English are taught in schools in the Middle East. In my country, however, students only graduated with a general understanding of the English alphabet and a few simple phrases. That was not adequate enough for my father. He wanted me to be fluent in English, an international language. He knew it would give me an excellent foundation for becoming a missionary to help spread Islam throughout the world.

In some countries in that region of the world, there are British and American schools that students can attend to learn English, among other things, but my father would not have sent me to one of those schools. Instead, he had Miss Claire come to our home, ostensibly to teach me English.

My country was not the only one in the region in which she taught. In fact, she taught in many "closed" countries, countries that are hostile to the teachings of Christ, countries in which Christians are persecuted.

From an early age, I broadly studied two areas. At my regular school, I studied academics. And at Islamic seminary, I studied Islamic theology, traditions, and Sharia law. Both were part of my life, though the emphasis was less on academics and more on seminary school. My teachers were all stern and firm. After many years of this, Miss Claire was a breath of fresh air. Quickly, perhaps instantly, she became my favorite teacher.

With Miss Claire, there was always a gigantic elephant in the room—love. I did not know what to do with it. Years later, I realized that so much of my questioning and unlearning stemmed from my time with her. It is often said of God that he goes deep within us to places that we are unaware of. He tackles our struggles that we do not even know we have. Grace is God as heart surgeon. He creates a renewed heart and a renewed mind in us.

Because she carried the fruit of the Holy Spirit and God's presence, Miss Claire brought that to every life she touched. I look back on how her presence alone was able to shift the atmosphere in a room, and I know that is how relevant I want to be in my life.

When I walk into a room, I want to transform the atmosphere. Like the disciples, I want my shadow to heal. We have been promised that we can accomplish greater things than we can possibly imagine, which means that miracles are a normal part of the Christian life.

Miss Claire was not simply a joyous reminder of life. She was also a lifeline and a healer. When I had a fever, Miss Claire would lay hands on me, and I would become well again.

As a child with post-traumatic stress disorder, I would occasionally "space out." If you looked at me, you would think I was staring at whatever was in front of me, but I was not daydreaming. Inside, my brain would be spinning, and my heart would be pounding as I replayed some aspect of the war. A bombing. Families blown to bits. Towns torn apart. Bloodshed. People screaming. The fear of death. I would lose the ability to speak.

Whenever that happened, Miss Claire knew I was not lost in my imagination. She knew how to end those episodes. She would hold me and whisper in my ear, "You're beautiful."

Looking back on those moments, I wonder what more she whispered under her breath. Bold prayers? Petitions to the Throne Room of Mercy and Grace?

Once when I was experiencing one of these episodes, Miss Claire giggled and said, "What's going on in that head of yours?"

I had been visualizing myself standing in the middle of a warzone and holding on to dozens of strings attached to enormous, colorful balloons.

Suddenly, I was lifted up into the sky. I flew high above the city. Away, away, away.

Out of his abundant love and grace, God put Miss Claire into my life. When she would pray in English, I did not understand everything she was saying.

Many years ago, my teacher, my lifeline, passed on. By faith, I believe that she is part of my cloud of witnesses. Yet, when I was young, I did not fully understand why she was in my life.

To me, Miss Claire is embodied in the following quote:[2]

> Your playing small does not serve the world. There is nothing enlightened about shrinking so that other people will not feel insecure around you. We are all meant to shine, as children do. We were born to make manifest the glory of God that is within us. It is not just in some of us; it is in everyone and as we let our own light shine, we unconsciously give others permission to do the same.
> **—Marianne Williamson**

I wonder, has there been a Miss Claire in your life? That is, has there been someone whom God was using to reach out to you, but you only realized that later?

Furthermore, I wonder, are you a Miss Claire in someone else's life? If you are, if you are trying to help someone find their own light, but that person is still lost in the darkness, it does not mean that God is not hearing and seeing you. It does not mean that God is not answering your prayers.

Over the decades, Miss Claire proved to me that each of us can be a carrier of seeds to a harvest we may never see. That is what she was for me. She planted seeds in me, yet she passed on before she saw the harvest in my life.

Miss Claire represented freedom.

She brought me joy.

She was gentle, kind, and caring.

She was gracious and graceful.

She encouraged me to dream and dream big.

Yet, I shared hundreds of ordinary moments with her.

I am convinced, years later, that God was using those common moments to make a difference in my life. He and Miss Claire were sprinkling seeds upon me and putting me in a safe place, without expecting anything in return, so that—when I was ready—I could grow. God and Miss Claire were patiently nurturing me with water, affection, happiness, protection, and perhaps most importantly, the light of unconditional love.

Miss Claire was even so bold as to share Jesus with my father. In doing this, she was a lioness speaking to a lion. Even though I have not revealed his identity to you, know this: for sharing Jesus with him, he could have had her head on a silver platter.

Many years later, on his deathbed, he came to know Jesus.

CHAPTER THREE

Marriage

Like many little girls, I adored weddings. The gorgeous makeup, opulent hairstyles, and lavish dresses. The delicious food. The singing and dancing. The beginning of a new chapter in life. And most importantly, the happy bride and groom. A couple in love, ready to start their lives together.

In traditional Islamic weddings, men and women spend the ceremony, including the dinner, in completely different venues. After dinner and some celebrating, women put on their hijabs, chadors, and abayas. Next, the groom gets into a decorated vehicle and drives to the lady's venue. Then he enters it to retrieve his wife. While this happens, all of the men wait outside. The parents of the bride and groom—or perhaps their siblings or best friends—help to cover the bride.

Then everyone gets into their own vehicle for a marriage procession that drives around the town or city. There is an abundance of honking, loud music, blocking traffic, and getting out of cars to dance in the middle of the street. It is a heartfelt celebration, with the community joining in the dancing and festivities, adding joy.

Like many girls, for years I dreamed of having a beautiful and extravagant wedding, but I did not just have high hopes for that marvelous day. I was not going to settle on just having a stunning ceremony. I wanted my marriage, my whole life with my husband, to be filled with happiness and based on love. That is what Miss Claire had taught me, after all: to dream big.

Unfortunately for me and the man who became my first husband, a fancy, blissful wedding followed by years of joy, affection, and passion was not meant to be.

My parents and my husband-to-be arranged my first marriage. Before I dive into the details, I want to be clear that my experience is solely that—it is *my story and my own* experience. Furthermore, I do not want this chapter to be just another standard sad story about a Middle Eastern girl forced to get married who then, by the skin of her teeth, somehow managed to escape.

This is important to emphasize because too often people hold unhelpful misconceptions and inaccurate stereotypes about arranged marriages, especially those in the Islamic faith. They mistakenly think that all arranged marriages have the same ingredients: the mean parents, the reluctant bride, the exchange of dowries, and the miserable, loveless life. They mistakenly assume that all arranged marriages are forced marriages, which is often not the case. My belief is that each marriage is unique in its own way, even the arranged ones.

I was married off at fourteen years old, making mine a

child marriage based on the predominant Western view of matrimony and the age of consent. By contrast, in the country of my birth, girls can be married after entering puberty. With that custom etched into us, child marriage is not automatically shunned like it is in most Western countries. There, in that particular Muslim culture, it is socially acceptable. That is why thousands of young girls are wed annually through arranged marriages.

Still, countless women in that society could choose whom they wanted to marry. They never experienced what I experienced. For instance, my own mother and most of my friends did not go through what I went through.

In short, I am trying to say that there is no one kind of love story.

I was extremely anxious.

I knew almost nothing about him.

I was about to marry a man whom I had never even met before.

Who was my future husband?

Would our marriage become the best and most beautiful thing in our lives?

I soon discovered this was not the man for me. In my moment of realization and epiphany, I decided I was going to take a stance and not agree to be married. In that moment, which was still a few months prior to the scheduled wedding, I put up a polite resistance to everything matrimonial. I told my parents, kindly, that I did not want to marry this man. I did not know him. I did not love him. In the beginning, I made civil comments such as: "Just in case you did not hear me, I actually am not agreeing to this." Things dragged on for what seemed like eternity. Gradually, though, I changed my approach.

I felt imprisoned. I felt unheard. I felt invisible. Nothing made sense. I just could not imagine my future "till death do us part" as a part of this equation. I had attended so many jubilant and stunning weddings, yet I was supposed to marry a man I had not even met. Who was going to dare stand against my father and advocate for me?

In my culture, marriages were often arranged, but they were not always forced upon sons and daughters. Instead, sons and daughters could, if they did not feel something for their intended fiancé or fiancée, wiggle out of the arrangement. They could say, "I don't care that the dowry took place. Here's your dowry back. I changed my mind." Then both sets of parents would have to restart the partner hunt.

My parents chose not to take that route. For them, it was a done deal. For me, there was no way out. They had my future planned out. I could say no to my parents regarding other things, but not this. Shame filled the air.

The prospect of marrying this man started affecting my mental health. I became depressed. I lost my appetite. I dwelled on negative feelings. I cried at random things. Anything even remotely stressful would shake my world.

On my wedding night, when it was time to take me to my new home, I hugged my dad as I was dropped off at my husband's house. I held him harder than I had ever held him before and pleaded with him, in a deep cry, "Baba, please...."

A principle I always live by is honor. Living an honorable life is crucial, partly because of the culture in which I was raised and partly because of the spiritual principle "we reap what we sow." To live by integrity is crucial to me. As best I can, I live my life doing what is right and being honest, fair, respectful, and loyal. All of these practices are wrapped up within the concept of honor.

With that in mind, I will not say anything untoward about my first husband. I will tell you that he was ambitious and wanted to follow in my father's footsteps. That he was the son my father never had. That he filled a void in Baba's life. But I will not speak unfavorably of my first husband. However, this point took a couple of years to get over.

Marriage is sacred. Marriage is holy. And divorce was something that my father did not approve of. Also, in Islam, divorce is greatly frowned upon for a woman. However, a divorced man can easily move on with life. Yes, our marriage was against my will. I never consented. But that has to be tempered with honoring my father.

Certainly, my Heavenly Father brought me out of it, and it *was* a miracle that I was able to leave that marriage. Still, even though my first husband sinned against me, even though he trespassed, at the end of the day, I want to be careful with my words.

I wonder, have I trespassed against someone? Have I dishonored someone? Have I hurt someone deeply? Yes, I have. And the first one I truly hurt was my Lord and Savior, Jesus Christ. I denied him.

During those years of my first marriage, I was afraid. I

was controlled. I was intimidated by the chauvinistic society. And yet, my former husband and I often had very frank conversations, such as: "Why would you want to be married to somebody who does not want to be married to you?"

I could not turn to anybody. There were no marriage therapists. I could not join a group that helped new wives deal with their new lives. These were options open to everyone else, but not to me because of who I was and because of the prestige of my family. There was nobody I could talk with because eventually my parents would find out about it.

In that culture, if a husband is unhappy with his marriage, he does not have to divorce his first wife; he can just marry another. Or two. Or three. Those options are not available to wives. Divorce is technically available to women, but in some particular cases, only men can initiate divorce proceedings. Furthermore, there are many substantial cultural barriers and legal hurdles that women must break down or leap over if they want a divorce. These difficulties simply do not exist for men wanting divorces.

For instance, if a woman wants to divorce, she has to give up her dowry, which is her insurance for survival. And if she is a mother, she has to give up her children. This is because under Islamic law, the custody of children is automatically awarded to the father. The husband also keeps all shared property. The wife must give up her rights to children, property, and all other financial assets.

In my former marriage, I realized that I was afraid. I was under immense pressure, and society's expectations weighed heavily upon me.

The following quote from Tony Reinke's book *Newton on the Christian Life: To Live Is Christ* relates to my feelings as I look back on that time of my life:[3]

> His grace cannot be exhausted (Matthew 14:13–21). His "unsearchable riches" are sufficient for millions of distressed sinners at the same time. Christ is a sun, he is an endless feast, and he is an endless ocean in breadth, length, height, and depth of unsearchable love (Ephesians 3:18–19).

Through my trials and challenges, through my emotional and physical pain, I have learned to pursue the truth within the storm. Christ's strength is found in my human weakness. Christ is a friend, the One who will not turn on you, will not walk away from you. I know God is faithful. I know he is working for my good.

Just because all of this happened when I was 14 does not mean it is not happening to girls around the world, even to girls in your neighborhood here in North America.

I have had the privilege of speaking in several different arenas in different capacities on topics to help better understand controversial matters with which Western culture struggles.

What I am about to share is a narrative based on true events. Names have been altered to protect the identities of the individuals involved. The commonality and frequency of such circumstances in our Western communities is many times higher than we hear on the news.

Mariam was born and raised in Canada. When she turned fifteen, her parents decided it was time for her to get married. One summer, her family decided to go home for a family reunion.

Coincidently, in speaking with a cousin back home, Mariam was informed that her parents were arranging a marriage for her and that she would remain in her home country and not return to Canada. She panicked, but she came up with a plan. She decided to put a spoon in her jean pocket and a fork in her purse. That way, when passing through airport security, she would be stopped and questioned. It worked. The spoon and fork triggered the metal detectors and got everyone's attention. She informed airport security that her husband was kidnapping her.

I am not certain what happened to Mariam's husband. However, Mariam was able to escape from her husband's control, and this quickly resulted in her family disowning her. Still a teenager and not yet a legal adult, she ended up in a foster home.

I was contacted through a church that was interested in helping Mariam. I met with her several times. I shared my story with her, just to give her some new perspectives on her tough and tragic situation. Unfortunately, I was not able to help Mariam in all the ways I wanted because the foster care system is not equipped to deal adequately with such unique situations.

Soon she was moved to a different foster home; this

one was a Christian home. I had high hopes. Yet, one day Mariam contacted me in tears. She had been raped by her foster brother.

I was furious. She had run away from a forced arranged marriage in her country of origin, only to be raped in a safe home, in a country that she believed would keep her safe.

Her parents started looking for her and contacted her friends. I visited her and came up with a few practical ways to stay safe and under the radar. She had to stop attending her high school. Another difficult process Mariam had to navigate was cutting ties with her friends.

"Are you kidding me?" she said to me. "I have already lost my family. Now you want me to lose my friends?"

"Well," I said, "do you not think it is possible for your parents to reach out to your best friend's family and ask them if they have heard from you? Mariam, do you think your mom and your friend's mom could have a heart-to-heart and, through tears and petition, possibly discuss your whereabouts?"

Beginning over again is extremely hard. It's not a simple or smooth process. It tugs at your heartstrings, uprooting ways of life that may have been in existence for decades, even since birth. Losses are weighed but not easily considered in comparison to the freedom waiting for us. It is extremely painful and difficult to take the steps necessary to achieve a safe end goal. Because change is so scary, it is easier to gravitate back to your comfort zone. Your judgment is easily clouded in the agony of loneliness and the fight to refind your way. We have all heard it said before: the best way to find yourself is to lose yourself.

Marriage without the consent of both parties involved is not a marriage. It is supposed to be a union, not a hijacking of someone's will. It can be complicated to move on, especially for a Muslim woman since there are several Sharia laws to navigate in order to receive an annulment.

The process that Mariam and I—and countless others before us and perhaps even after us—endure in some cutlural systems causes an outbreak, an earthquake in the soul. There is a need to rediscover identity and purpose. To find our purpose and destiny, there is a battle that we need to win. It happens in the breaking. In the dark, silent nights. In the crying out. In the searching. To start over again means to leave the bad behind and take with you only the good. To do what needs to be done in the moment and remain faithful to what has been set before you, keeping it balanced and consistent. Taking it bit by bit can take you a long way. But, taking that first step is just the beginning.

This journey of starting over requires *courage—lots of courage*. It is the key to this brave walk. You must have the courage to walk away from your nest, your comfort, your friends, and everything you once believed to be solid, constant, and true. One of my favorite authors and researchers is Brené Brown, who has said the following on this topic: "The key to whole-hearted living is vulnerability. You measure courage by how vulnerable you are."[4] She goes further to say that you can choose comfort or courage, but you cannot have both. Maya Angelou said, "Courage is the most important of all virtues because without courage, you can't practice any other virtues consistently."⁵

I believe that without courage one can miss out on living full-heartedly. This means being authentic and grateful and knowing your self-worth. To know that you are loved and seen is to be brave.

Perhaps you have been through a battle that caused you to question everything. Whether you are avoiding it or addressing it directly, know that fighting will make you stronger. If you are in the middle of your war today, keep going. You are a warrior. Every scar will bear witness to your hardship. Be proud of your scars. If you have made it through, you are an overcomer, a conqueror of everything the enemy has thrown at you.

Pericles once said, "The bravest are surely those who have the clearest vision of what is before them, glory and danger alike, and yet notwithstanding, go out to meet it."⁶

It is a daring journey to walk away from family roots that have held you together, taught you, and guided you to reach your current stance or viewpoint. Whether this was possible through your agreement or defiance, it still made you who you are today.

Marriage can be a battle, but a victorious one at that—all jokes aside.

Marriage is not a contract. It is a covenant.

It is not defined by age or race. It is not limited by culture or education. It often is not beautiful, but it is amazing. It is the most difficult, most rewarding job there is. It does not give up easily. It is not a prison, but it is a choice. It is the arguments, fits, and fights. It is the persistence to stay committed to one another. It is the laughing, the endless laundry, the imperfections that you want to live without but will not live without. Marriage is breaking bread together and getting drunk on joy.

Marriage is loving when the other is seriously imperfect or unlovable.

Marriage is one Heaven of a ride. Then why did I end up divorced? Because I never agreed to it to begin with.

Marriage is not easy. It is hard work, and that is life.

Marriage is a holy union, with God at the center (2 Corinthians 6:14). It is "gentle and humble in heart" (Matthew 11:29). Marriage is sacrificial love (Ephesians 5:25) and hopes in the Lord (Romans 10:11). It is certainly forgiving (1 Corinthians 13:5), remembering that everyone needs grace (Ephesians 2:8).

CHAPTER FOUR

Trauma and Healing

Life is meant to be lived. It is messy and painful. One season is a celebration, and the next, can turn into agony.

In the process of growing up at home and perhaps moving out to university to find yourself, your identity, and passions, you experience the uphill battles when you can hardly breathe. These may turn out to be the years that shape your faith, the anchor that brings you to your knees. It can be the time when you find love or a friend for life. However small or significant the journey turns out to be, there is a transformative power to create meaning and thrust us forward.

Others may not experience moving out because they were selfishly kept in a cage when they were meant to spread their wings and fly.

How are the heroes separated from the strong? The heroes bear their losses, pick up their shield, and fight a good fight. As Bob Richards once said, "It may sound strange, but many champions are made champions by setbacks."

Setbacks, defeat, sweat, and blood are part of every traumatic journey. It simply varies from one person to the next. For me, basements are a particular place that can provoke my trauma. When I was little, our house had an enormous basement that had been converted into a mini hospital. Whenever the air-raid sirens would wail in our city, we would turn off every light in the house and descend into our very own underground hospital. Over the years, wounded soldiers would be brought to our home to be treated. Our home, our basement, our mini hospital.

But my trauma, to be frank, is much more complex than just basements. One of the most disturbing memories I have of being a child relates to watching a military funeral procession pass by that contained a "sea of bodies." Often, processions for soldiers killed in the war were organized. Thousands of people would gather to pay their respects and patriarchy. I witnessed many of these processions. During one of them, I was perched on my auntie's shoulders. I was sitting on top of her chador or abaya as I held on to her head.

All around us, there were bodies everywhere being carried by mourners, but the corpses were not in coffins. They were wrapped in white burial shrouds. For many of them who had recently been transported from battlefields, blood was seeping through their shrouds.

In Islamic culture, it is an honor to touch martyrs because they are going straight to Heaven. Since martyrdom represents the highest achievement attainable by a Muslim, if you touch a martyr, it is as if their glory might rub off on you.

There were thousands of people weeping and wailing,

mourners not holding any emotions back. There were hundreds of dead bodies wrapped in bloody shrouds, with mourners reaching up and touching them. Touching their brothers, their husbands, their fathers. A seemingly endless sea of bodies.

Many Middle Easterners have grown up with war. For people in the West who have not grown up in war, I want to provide a little thought experiment that may put our experience into perspective. Before I do that, though, I want to be clear that what I am about to say is not meant to minimize or delegitimize anyone's personal experience. Without a doubt, everyone's individual experience of war is valid. That said, here is my idea.

On September 11, 2001, thousands of people lived in close proximity to the Twin Towers. After terrorists crashed planes into those buildings, thousands of people continued to live near that part of downtown Manhattan. That is, they lived near the few city blocks that became known as Ground Zero. In the months after the attacks, as best they could, those New Yorkers continued on with their lives.

Now try to imagine the small geographic area of New York's Ground Zero being your entire country, but not just for a short period of time, for many years. In a horribly concrete way, that was what it was like growing up in a war-ravaged country.

There was war on *every* block.

At any moment, you knew that war could catch up with you.

Fear was omnipresent. People died travelling to work.

One day, a school would be standing on a particular block. The next day, there would be a smoldering crater in the playground, and you would wonder how many children were killed.

But you adjusted. You tried your best to go on with your life. You mourned, and you moved on. That became your reality. It became *life*. There was still music in the air, but occasionally there were also air-raid sirens.

For a long while, I did not know I had post-traumatic stress disorder. I was not aware that there was a name for what I was experiencing. I knew I was sad. I knew I was hurting. But I figured that since everyone gets sad and everyone hurts, my sadness and hurt were normal.

When I look back on those times when trauma paralyzed me, I think, *"How many other people are going through the same thing I experienced—or worse?"*

How do we overcome trauma? How can we be sensitive to other people's traumatic stories?

No one who listens to another person's traumatic story has the right to say, "Well, I don't think that is really traumatic." We must not dismissively say, "Didn't that happen to you when you were six? Can't you just get over it?" We should not assume that our personal bias regarding what trauma means is the same as another person's perspective.

In a similar vein, when we are at church, we must not say to people with trauma, "Don't you have enough faith? Don't you trust that God is going to heal you?" Those comments can be incredibly hurtful. Believe me, I know. People have levelled them at me.

I have even had someone say to me, "I can only imagine what you have gone through." But that is not true. They cannot imagine what I have gone through. It would be better if that person had said the exact opposite: "I can't imagine what you have gone through."

I have seen war. I have lived through it. It is your city being constantly bombed. It is losing loved ones.

I believe that we can experience healing by telling our stories and by recognizing the traumas.

When I am feeling sad or miserable, I think of myself as being "gray." Sometimes when I am like that, a family member may continue to laugh or smile when they are around me. When they choose not to let my gray rain on them, their joy and laughter begin to move into my atmosphere and pull me out of that dark cloud.

There are commonalities that we have to find within humanity. No matter what color we are. No matter which culture we are from. No matter our religion and faith.

It can be an organic human experience to sit together and listen to each other's stories. Listening with empathy is powerful.

Soon after I escaped a war zone, I was at Heathrow airport. Covered head to toe, I met a stranger. She said to me, "I'm glad you're here." She did not ask me intrusive questions. She did not confront me with a wall of pity. She *saw* me. She *heard* me. I was immeasurably grateful.

There were years when I rarely shared my story. Sometimes when I thought it was safe to share, I would face criticism. Often that criticism was painful. Then I would have to deal with that criticism in addition to my own trauma.

Telling your story is not always restorative.

We are all broken. Some people are too broken to relate. They do not have the will to say, "I have been there."

But you have to keep trying to find the right moment and the right listener.

It has taken me many years to process my trauma. I am still processing it. Healing, for me, came wave after wave. I have been the victim, but I am no longer the victim.

Gradually, my feelings of humiliation and hostility are subsiding.

Gradually, my unhelpful beliefs about certain events in my life are diminishing.

Gradually, my painful memories are having less power over me.

I am coping.

I am making sense of it all.

Sometimes with trauma, it is hard to know where to draw the line between "this is physiological" and "this is spiritual."

CHAPTER FIVE

Identity and Labels

When you read the Bible deeply, you will find that our identity in Christ is mentioned all throughout the Good Book. Each of those verses undeniably speaks to our character, personality traits, qualities, beliefs, and even the strong link between the person and his Maker. All of this is magnificently knitted with our personal identity and our identity in Christ.

Being a refugee is seeking refuge, seeking a safe place. You do not have friends. You do not have a home. You have lost everything. Even when you lay your head down at a refugee camp, there is no chance that you will rest.

My identity as a refugee was a remarkably broken identity. It was almost entirely subjective. Living moment to moment, I was completely unanchored.

My identity was fear. It was survival mode. It was carrying my trauma everywhere I went.

I was in pain.

I was angry.

When I was a refugee, since I had run out of options,

all I could do was run and pray. When I was praying, though, it was not about me as a person, what I had accomplished, what I had failed at. It was about a God who wanted me and you before He even created us. I am talking about a God who came looking for me—and for you—and said that no matter what I was going through, he would work it for my good.

He chose me. I have been subjected to a lot of brokenness in this world, but I have a God who yearns for me.

God was a Father before he was a Creator. That same Father is the one who created me and adopted me. He called me. He opened my eyes so that I would be humbled and crumbled enough to say, "Okay, I give up. I can't do this on my own." That is how he revealed himself—through the Holy Spirit.

Suffering is temporary. Victories are eternal and permanent. I know there are promises that I can stand on firmly and forever, promises that will never change. These include the promise that I am not alone, the promise that he will never leave me or forsake me (Deuteronomy 31:6; Hebrews 13:5; Matthew 28:20). I have never had promises like that from any god I have served. Those are extremely confirming, affirming, and anchoring promises.

Start believing what God says about you. Memorize the promises of God. Read the affirmations God has given you. Write them in a notebook. Read them aloud to yourself. Allow yourself to hear your own voice reading the powerful promises God has written about you. Let them penetrate you. Let them sink in.

Then listen to the Holy Spirit. Listen to the still voice

that affirms the Word of God. He is the Comforter. He is confirming. He is your teacher and your guide. Stop giving the enemy a say in your life. Pause and put him on mute. In fact, delete his file completely.

The devil cannot hurt God, but he can hurt God's children. So that is precisely what the despicable enemy does—he goes after God's children. Satan has never created anything, and he never will. His mission is to kill, steal, and destroy (John 10:10).

One tool that the enemy uses is the words of others. Sometimes it is what your parents speak over you. Sometimes it is your friends or community trying to shape you into something you are not, something outside of how God wants to mold you in his image. Those labels can be hurtful. They can create bitterness and anger. They can create cultures that are not aligned with Jesus' culture.

I have had the honor and privilege of speaking at churches and universities, and there have been occasions when I would see a woman in the audience crying because she could relate to being raped or being trafficked or experiencing domestic violence. You may know someone like that. You yourself might even have personally experienced those inhumanities. If so, I would sit with you and say, "There's no magic pill. But there is a lifeline. And there's One who collects every tear. His name is Jesus, and he promises that he will be there. In fact, he is beside you right now."

Throughout our lives, labels get placed on us. Without our permission, people—sometimes strangers, sometimes loved ones—sneak up on us and glue their labels onto us.

These labels can add up and weigh down our identity. For years, they can be a source of pain. Every time you hear a particular word, you cringe because you know that someone once marked you with it.

Nowadays, in our hectic world, people are occasionally labelled with their job titles. A successful business person may be the Chief Executive Officer of a prosperous company. But is CEO their whole identity? Furthermore, is their identity based on how effective they are at accumulating wealth?

No, of course not.

But you would be surprised at how many people—perhaps you, too—get mistakenly pigeonholed by their past.

Sometimes our identity can get mixed up with what others tell us about who we are. In the past, person-to-person and other physical interactions were the primary form of communication and feedback. Today there is still an element of people-to-people communication, but also machine-to-people communication, all done through digital channels. With the myriad of digital exchanges and digital experiences we all have these days, it is easy to second-guess what we see online and what we see others doing or claiming to do.

What is real? What is not?

It is not hard to believe that we are possibly getting subjected to "fake news" and "alternative facts." What we do know for sure is that there are people online who want to take advantage of others through modern mediums.

When we spend too much time online, we get lost. We are constantly being bombarded by so many different options and varying points of view. All of it causes confusion. It makes us constantly second-guess our social status, our purpose, and who we really are. Those who cannot filter through the noise are setting themselves up for a lose-lose situation.

Just think about how hard it must be for kids to understand what is genuine and what is not. Most of the younger generation judge and perceive the world based largely on what they see online. There has to be an education, something simple and basic, to help girls and boys understand that what they see on social media is not necessarily what they need to become, that some virtual interactions and digital experiences risk negatively shaping their core purpose in life. They need to be given the tools to filter the good and the bad from everything coming at them today.

We can take a lighthearted approach to all of this. We can even laugh at it as we intellectually analyze our labels and what has shaped us. But how are we going to learn so that we can raise our children differently? How are we going to raise them so that they fully grasp that being a teenager is not about accruing likes on social media? How will we impart to them that being an adult should not be about how rich they become, what job they get, or what zip code they live in?

We cannot just ask our children broad questions—"Who are you?" and "What are you into?"—and then expect them to figure out their identity.

Maybe as parents, we need to ask ourselves a few questions first:

1. How do we support our children no matter what?
2. How do we encourage them to figure out who they are?
3. How do we both mold them and respect their wishes to be whoever they want to be?
4. What limits should we place on the hobbies and other things our children really like?
5. What guidance should we give to authority figures, like teachers and caregivers, who can shape the judgments and perceptions of our children?

I wish my parents would have asked themselves these kinds of questions when I was a child.

When I was nine, I felt so left out, so abandoned, that I decided I just had to be adopted. See, my family was really large, and one day I just figured out that I must be biologically unrelated to everyone else in our household.

All of this got even more confusing when I was twelve and my father sat me down. "I have all these sons and daughters," he said. "But you are the only one."

I thought he was confirming that I *had* been adopted. Kicking, crying, and screaming, I ran away from him.

Years later, I realized he was not telling me that I was a biological outcast, like a black sheep. Instead, he was telling me that I was more akin to a surprise or a wonder of God, like a black swan. That is, he was telling me that I was special, that I was his precious one, that I might even be his favorite.

So, what is truly the anchor of our identity? It is our Holy Trinity. It is our safe haven in Christ under the wings of our Father. He is our highest advocate in any court. It is essential that we know we have an advocate who is not only going to bail us out; he already paid for it all. He paid our debt.

No matter how many times my earthly father messed up, I have a Heavenly Father who will make up for it.

No matter how many times I felt orphaned or rejected by my parents, I have a Father who adopted me.

The anchor of our identity is in Christ.

We can find our identity in our brokenness.

We were created with an appetite to see the impossibilities in life and to bend our knees at the name of Jesus. He is the God of impossibilities made possible.

If you remove the lies, judgments, and unmet expectations and you face the devastation and brokenness, then you will find your purpose. When you confront these challenges, you can become the best version of yourself.

But it does not stop there. Our purpose includes reaching out to people around us who have experienced catastrophes of war, loss, and rejection. God has placed specific individuals around you and in your life, and none of it is by accident. Pay attention and help them to overcome what you have already conquered in your life.

Years ago, my identity was anger. In the past, when I witnessed something dreadful perpetrated against someone, I would want to pick up my sword. I would not want to turn the other cheek and be weak, yet that is what is required.

The Kingdom of God does not label people. It does not say, "You're Buddhist" or "You're Hindu" or "You're Muslim." The Kingdom of God does not say, "Because of who you are, I am not going to stand up for you."

The Kingdom of God is about love.

Kill them with love—that is the kind of slogan I now live by.

If I stand up in Christ—in his Kingdom way—it looks very different. His Kingdom is upside down. It is the last who will be first (Matthew 19:30, 20:16). It is the one who gives the most who will be the richest.

When I think about how people find their identity, I think of the following quote by Blaise Pascal: "Not only do we know God only through Jesus Christ, but we know ourselves only through Jesus Christ. We know life, death, only through Jesus Christ. Except by Jesus Christ, we know not what our life is, what our death is, what God is, what we are ourselves."[7]

When it comes to our identity, it is often hard for us to distinguish what we are, yet it is sometimes easy to figure out what we are *not*.

Think back to your childhood. Remember all the times you were asked, "What do you want to be when you grow up?" Some people knew what they wanted to be. I remember when my son was about four years old and someone asked him, "What do you want to be when you grow up?" He went quiet, unsure if his answer was okay or not. Then he put on a brave smile and said, "I want to be a father when I grow up!" I love it, the certainty, the absolute desire. And without a doubt, we heard him loud and clear: my son wanted to be the best dad he could be.

And does not this world need fathers? That would be a job that is up there with the superheroes.

Some may not know their full identity in Christ, but we know where to find it.

Jesus Christ has accepted us as we are, but he loves us too much to leave us there.

In our human life, we can experience all manner of rejection. Rejection from when we were children and were continuously picked last on the playground. Rejection that causes deep soul wounds. We can be rejected by our families. Rejected by universities or places of work. Rejected by a loved one.

The only way to heal those types of wounds is to find acceptance in our lives, to feel included, favored, and wanted. The journey to finding that acceptance can lead to wrong turns and dark alleys. Some of us return to the places we once experienced rejection, only to find that nothing has changed and rejection still reigns.

The good news is that you do not need to seek acceptance from an elite group, from a parent who was too broken to love you the way you needed to be loved, or from a friend who used you. The ultimate truth is that regardless of where you are in your journey called life, and regardless of how many players are at the table with you, *you have been chosen by God, who loves you with a divine, undying love.*

CHAPTER SIX

Perseverance

I have had to restart my life so many times.

These were not simple moments when I said to myself, *"Okay, how can I refocus in my life? Okay, let's brainstorm."* No. I am talking about moving countries. I am talking about leaving my identity behind. I am talking about everything in my life crumbling and having to rebuild myself from scratch.

In those moments, there was enormous pain. I would keep telling myself, *"I will get up. I will stand again. I will move forward. I will overcome these fears. I can see hope. I can see the light."*

Those days were my own personal Ground Zero. I do not want to insult anyone by using that term, nor am I trying to diminish or offend the memories of the September 11 attacks. It is just that this term—"my own personal Ground Zero"—accurately captures how I feel about those dark days of my past.

In the shattered and dangerous moments of our lives, we have to choose perseverance. We have to recover. We have to adjust. Despite all of the difficulties confronting us, we have to continue striving. We have to build upon yesterday, build today, build for tomorrow.

After I left—escaped—the Middle East, I moved into an apartment that was in a little town next to a beach. I tried to get settled. I tried to focus on the positive, such as how my boys and I had moved to a new neighborhood that we could explore. But there was so much working against us. It was winter, but we did not have appropriate clothing to keep us warm. The floors in our apartment were concrete, making the whole apartment extremely cold.

We had only one chair in the living room and one sheet for each bed. We did not have blankets or pillows, sweaters or jackets.

I just locked myself in that apartment, and I was so angry.

"I am done with you!" I yelled at Allah. "I do not know what else you want from me. I have done everything I know how to do. To the best of my abilities, I have done everything you have asked me to do, and it seems I am not getting it right. What am I doing wrong?"

We barely had any food in the house.

I said to Allah, "I am going to fast for you."

I took my lack of food and not having a choice, and I decided to give it to Allah. I decided that I would not eat until he fed me, so I started fasting.

On the third day of my fast, there was a knock at my front door. My children were really excited, but I was thinking, *"I probably shouldn't even open the door because it does not matter. None of this matters. Whoever it is, they probably have the wrong house. Nobody knows me in this town. Nobody knows to look for me here."*

Then my paranoia kicked in.

"Should I open the door?"

Eventually, my curiosity got the best of me, and I decided to see who it was. I put on my hijab. I opened the door. Three people stood there: a mother, a father, and their son. I felt a wave of joy wash over me.

It was obvious to me that they were a family. I instantly thought of the rest of my family back in the Middle East and how I might never see them again, and I started to cry.

I was embarrassed and ashamed.

All through my bones, I knew what these three people were doing. In the past, I had been them. I had carried food, clothing, and toys, and I had knocked on the doors of strangers just like them. But today, I was not the giver; I was the receiver. They were here for me and my children.

The man mentioned my name and asked if I was that person. If someone knows my name, it is usually a red flag. Who I was in the Middle East—whose daughter I was—contributed to why I had to leave that life behind me. But when he asked me who I was and said my real name, I answered, "Yes, I am."

"We brought your food," the woman said.

They went to their car and brought back over thirty bags of groceries.

I let them in. The food completely filled my tiny kitchen and previously empty fridge.

I brought them into the living room, where there was only one chair. The mother sat on it. She looked at me and said, "Would you like us to put you in touch with the

Muslim community?"

I had a kind of meltdown. I just lost it. "No," I yelled at her, "I do not want to be a part of the Muslim community here."

Prior to that moment in my life, I had never been angry towards my people. I was angry because if it had not been for my people, I would not have been forced to run away from my life in the Middle East. It was the first time I ever pointed the finger the other way, *not* at Americans. It was a eureka moment, an epiphany, a revelation. When I told this matriarchal figure that I was uninterested in being part of the Islamic community here in town, I was essentially saying that I was willing to be alone.

You have to understand that Muslims do not exist alone. If you are Muslim, you are always part of a community. That is a permanent part of your identity. If someone asks a Muslim person, "Who are you?" it is common for them to respond, "I am Muslim. My name is ___ ," and then say their name. That is who you are.

And there I was, standing in my own unadorned, sparse living room, talking with strangers about my identity and not wanting to be part of my own community. Why on earth would I do that?

I did not know it at the time, but something broke in me. I was rejecting my tribe.

The mother just sat there peacefully, her husband and son standing on either side of her. She came at me with the heart of God, with the motherhood of God. She said to me, "I can tell you are strong. But you have to be stronger because of your boys. You are safe now. You are okay.

You will be fine. You do not have to fear." Then she added, "Can we pray for you in Jesus' name?"

If you do not know that much about Islam, you may assume that Muslims would respond to such a request by saying, "No, definitely do not pray for me in Jesus' name!" Yet, generally, Muslims will receive prayers in Jesus' name, so that is what I did. I said, "Yes."

"God does not have an agenda," she said. "He just comes to you with love." After saying that, she prayed that I would sleep, that I would feel his peace, that I would feel his joy all over my life. But she did not stop there. She went on and on and on, praying for everything that I was struggling with.

After she and her family had prayed for me, the mother asked, "Would you be open to coming to a gathering? We host it at our house. It is for single parents." Then she added, "Maybe you'll meet somebody…."

I remember thinking, *"I definitely do not want to meet anybody. No, thank you."*

But before I could speak, she told me about how this group was helping her daughter, who was a single mother like me. As she continued to talk about this "gathering," I figured out that she was actually talking about a Bible study group for young adults. She explained how parents could come with their children, how she had a playroom, and how there were veggies and dip. I agreed.

Just before the family left my apartment, the husband gave me his card. He had not mentioned his career before, but his card made it clear—he was the chief of police. I thought, *"This must be a sign from God. I am protected. If I am ever afraid or attacked, I can contact him. He'll help me."*

It is funny to me now that I focused on that instead of focusing on how God had provided for me. Sometimes we do that. We focus on miniscule things that are ultimately meaningless, and we miss the big picture right in front of our very eyes of how much God, behind the scenes, is doing for us right now.

I had been spending too much time indoors.

But that day, everything turned upside down. There I was, putting my life in the hands of this compassionate family. But God was right there, too, and I had not been paying attention to his presence in my life. He had held my hand and taken me to this new Western country. He had guided those magnanimous strangers to knock on my door. He had brought me all of those bags of groceries. He had given me the energy to say yes to the mother's invitation.

But everything I have just described, which is now obvious to me, is only clear because—you know what they say—hindsight is 20/20. However, during that transitional period, everything was murky. Around every corner, mayhem lurked; clarity was a fallacy. It was not as if I had lived through all of that trauma, was finished with feeling frustrated and angry, and wanted to open up to God and say, "God, I want to persevere and see what you have in store for me."

No. I was not like that at all.

I was done with God.

I wanted to see what I could achieve without him.

I was rejecting God.

You would think that at a time like that, I would want to put more trust in him. Not so. I wanted to put my trust in the three people who had just come into my cold, empty apartment and left it warmer and fuller. I was not going to trust God anymore.

I had such a massive chip on my shoulder; I know that now. Everything was about yours truly—*me, myself, and I*. Well, come to think of it, everything was about me except taking responsibility for myself. See, at that low point in my life, I blamed God for pretty much everything. For everything else, I blamed politics, religion, friends, and family.

Let's get back to my three "wise men" who knocked on my door and whom I invited into my empty home. A few days later, they came again to visit. This time, however, it was Sunday, and they were picking me up to take me to Sunday service.

That is when the strangest thing happened. I was doing my hair and was about to put on my hijab, and I suddenly felt like I had permission to go outside without my head covering, which prior to then I had worn most of my life. This was a pivotal moment to say the least. For all of my life, it had been understood that men could only look at women sexually. In response, we Muslim women had to cover ourselves. It was our job to protect ourselves from men's desire because our bodies caused chaos within men.

Yet, on my doorstep were the police chief and his son, and I somehow knew that they were not going to look at me sexually. So I decided not to wear the hijab.

They drove me and my boys to church.

We arrived at church, and I felt that I had perhaps

entered a different dimension. I had never let my boys out of my sight, yet as soon as we walked through those church doors, I felt a wave of love. I knew we were safe.

I fell to my knees, and I cried. I sobbed. I wept.

Looking back now, I could see Jesus being there. I was at his feet, washing his precious feet with my tears and drying his feet with my long, thick hair. My alabaster box was my alabaster heart.

I was mourning the death of my old self. I had never cried nor mourned that way before.

I was safe. I was home.

The presence of the Holy Spirit was a tsunami full of a love and a peace that I had not met before.

That day, I changed. I was never going to be the same again. I had met the One whom I had missed with my very existence. How could I miss a person I had never met? But it was effortless. The Father, Jesus, and the Holy Spirit—together, intertwined. I was held together by justice, mercy, love, and grace. I could not breathe; I was like a newborn. And I cried for more of him.

When I came back to reality from that supernatural realm, it was the music that grabbed my attention. I thought, *"This is exactly what I have been looking for. This. Right here. Right now. This is what I have been searching for ever since I was 17."* Mind you, when I was 17, there was no way I even contemplated changing my religion, but I knew I was searching for something. And then I found it. I was worshipping in Spirit and in Truth. It was the worship music and the singing. The concentrated corporate anointing drew me in deeper. I could almost hear the angels singing in the room: "'Holy, holy,

holy is the Lord God Almighty,' who was, and is, and is to come" (Revelation 4:8).

That is when I experienced yet another watershed moment. I realized that I could listen to the music and the singing, and everything would be fine. That may be common sense to you, but it was monumental for me. The incredible music and beautiful voices were breathtaking. Wondrous and life-affirming, it was like I had walked into a magical place, and I could hear angels playing instruments and saints singing. I was in awe—which makes sense because that day I met the Holy Spirit.

In the church, the service was coming to an end. I was sincerely surprised. It was only about one and a half hours long. *"I am not done,"* I thought. *"I am undone. I want more. Could we stay longer?"* As a former Muslim who attended mosque, I was accustomed to gatherings that rarely lasted less than three hours and often as long as six hours. Everyone in the community would come together, not just to pray and gather around a message, but also to prepare food together and share a meal together. However, my new life was—abruptly—starting, and I had to get on everyone else's page.

Later that day when I was at home, I still wanted to go back to church. That one experience was not enough for me, by any means. It was a lifeline. It fed me, and it was like nothing I had ever tasted or seen. I could not get enough of it. Over the next few months, I still wanted more. Sure, I went to Bible study once a week, and I went to service every Sunday. But I wanted more of God.

I began seeking the Living Word, the living God. He was so quick to answer, so available, so near. I had his attention, and he had mine. I was discovering a deeper meaning. I was beginning "to grasp how wide and long and high and deep is the love of Christ, and to know this love that surpasses knowledge—that you may be filled to the measure of all the fullness of God. Now to him who is able to do immeasurably more than all we ask or imagine, according to his power that is at work within us, to him be glory in the church and in Christ Jesus throughout all generations, for ever and ever! Amen" (Ephesians 3:18–21).

Looking back at my journey with God, it is amazing to me how patient he is. He is after our hearts. He knew that I was searching, that I was broken. He knew that I wanted to do the right thing. So he just walked with me. All of those years of my life when I was praying to Allah, I now know that Yahweh was listening.

I love how God comes into our lives without an agenda. *We* have agendas, but God just wants to listen to us and to love us.

CHAPTER SEVEN

Prayer and Miracles

I love praying. Prayer has been my lifeline, and it has been my miracle.

Prayer does not keep us from having problems. It just provides us with a different view of how God is responding to our problems.

Through prayer, I have personally witnessed many miracles.

In this chapter, I will share various anecdotes and insights from my life that reveal the exquisite interconnectedness of prayer and miracles.

Sometimes when our ego gets in the way, we completely miss miracles that are happening right in front of us. Worse, sometimes we impede miracles.

When I was in grade four in the Middle East, there was a girl my age who had a medical issue with her throat. (Let's call her Mercy.) One day, Mercy asked me, "Can I sing the Adhan today?"

As you may know, every day of a Muslim's life is punctuated with five ritual prayers. The call to prayer reminds Muslims to stop, pause, and pray, to leave worldly matters behind. At school, I sang the Adhan.

"No," I replied to Mercy.

"Come on, please," Mercy begged.

I shook my head. "Even when you talk normally, it is like your voice disappears. You will never be able to do the call to prayer properly."

Ouch. Girls can be mean, but I was brutal.

I was also being truthful. As the saying goes, the truth sometimes hurts. With her throat condition, she would never be able to sing a beautiful version of the Islamic call to prayer.

Months later, I was about to go on a trip with my family, and Mercy came to me. "I know you never let me say the call to prayer," she said. "And I know I am not worthy of saying the Adhan. Your voice is so beautiful. So I just want to ask for your forgiveness. Also, when you get to wherever you are going, at the first shrine you visit, would you please say a prayer for me?"

Now, decades later, I can see her heart posture. But back then, I was ignorant of it because I was standing in my ego, my humanness. I was unaware that she was really asking me if I would let her call out to God so that she could be healed.

I pray that Mercy has been healed so she can sing to Christ, so she can call out to the living God. I pray that she has her voice so that she can share her own miraculous story.

I once led a workshop that I intentionally created for both Christians and non-Christians. I did not want it to be solely for Christians because I also wanted it to speak to skeptics, agnostics, and maybe even atheists, too.

In one of the breaks in the workshop, a Buddhist couple came up to me. (Let's call them Mr. and Mrs. Zhang.)

"We can see something in you," Mr. Zhang said.

"What do you mean?" I said.

"Your aura," Mrs. Zhang said. "Have you heard of auras? Have you heard of colors?"

I nodded.

Then, from out of nowhere, Mr. Zhang said, "You have the ability to heal."

I thought, *"Sure, Jesus is a healer, and I carry him within."* But I did not say anything. I just waited politely.

"We have been married for about twelve years," Mrs. Zhang said. "We have been trying to have children for about ten years. Would you pray for us?"

"Yes, definitely," I said. And I thought, *"I can bless you. Yes, absolutely. Blessings are freely given."*

We went into a private room. They got down on their knees. I sat with crossed legs. We formed a nice circle, and I could not help thinking, *"I am Middle Eastern. My new friends are Asian. If someone could see us right now, they'd probably think this is one massive clash of cultures."* But if someone ever thought that about us, they would be missing the point. That moment was not about cultures. It was people coming together with God to make impossibilities possible.

They had asked me to bless them, so I started off by saying, "Is it okay if I pray for you in Jesus' name?"

"Jesus is good," Mrs. Zhang said. "We believe in Jesus. We believe in all gods."

"Oh, God," I thought. "All right," I said, "so let's go with Jesus. Let's pick him."

I blessed them. I began praying the heart of the Father over them, and they both began to cry.

Then, after getting her permission, I laid my hands on Mrs. Zhang's womb and started speaking to her womb.

Flash forward a year later, and the Zhangs emailed me that they were expecting twins!

I was over the moon. When you hear that you have prayed for someone and God used that prayer, it really touches you.

I think it is important for us to update our understanding of miracles. It is almost as if we need to redefine what we think of as miracles. God delicately interacts with us via other people, though at the time, we may be oblivious to his presence.

I am in awe of how God brings people with Muslim backgrounds out of the Middle East and into various countries around the world, including Canada, the U.S., the U.K., and many other countries. This is part of a wave of conversions from Islam to Christianity that is currently sweeping the world. This widespread conversion cannot just be explained away by saying that there are now more Bible translations in colloquial languages that are spoken by Muslims. These spiritual transformations cannot just be explained away by saying that the internet is a major factor in exposing Muslims to Christianity. No. It is much more than all of that. It is a modern miracle that neither science nor technology can come close to explaining.

One of the most profound miracles I ever personally

experienced relates to when I left a Middle Eastern country to start a new life.

I landed in a foreign country. The airport was gigantic. Ceilings as high as the sky. Massive steel girders and concrete walls. Noisy conveyor belts and beeping carts.

I obviously was not alone. There were travellers everywhere—weary parents, crying babies—and armed guards. But there's a difference between aloneness and loneliness. I felt the loneliest I have ever felt in my life. I felt completely powerless.

In my home country, I had often been called brave. Various people, in times of depression and oppression, sought me out for help and protection. But in this brave new world, far from everything I had ever known, I did not feel brave at all.

For most of my life up to that point, my identity had been firm. I knew who I was. I was not just mentally strong. Back home, I was protected. I was a member of an immensely influential family, and my father was one of the most powerful men in the country. In a way, I had a level of immunity.

But at that airport, after I left my home country for good, God allowed me to be broken.

I realized that I *had been* somebody, but now I was a nobody.

Almost everything I had was gone in a moment.

My family—gone.

My confidence—gone.

My protection—gone.

My identity—who was I?

Suddenly, I was on my own. My father would not be

able to protect me. *Nobody* would be able to protect me.

In that ruthless, painful airport, it was now my turn to experience the unknowns.

I looked around at the people nearby.

I saw people standing in circles and huddles. They had each other's backs.

I saw young couples that were afraid of being robbed of their only precious possession—love. They were in a world of their own. I could see hope in their eyes. They had nothing to hide. No matter the cost, they would confess their love on the world stage. Their love was the kind of love that A. B. Simpson wrote about over one hundred years ago: "[t]he love that cannot help but love; loving, like God, for the very sake of love."[8]

If any of the people I was noticing happened to notice me, they probably thought that I appeared calm and collected. But inside of this little girl, a desert storm was raging. Indeed, within a few short minutes, the sandstorm was all around me. Sand blinding me. Sand choking me. Under my abaya—the cloak that millions of Muslim women wear—my skin was pins and needles. There was nowhere to go, nowhere to hide. Even if I had put my hand in front of my face, I would not have been able to see it.

Anxiety hit hard. I just wanted to sit. I wanted to lie down and sleep my worries away, but I had no safe place to go. I could not hear, but the voices in my head were clear. The emptiness felt lonely.

There was one thing that enabled me to break free from that sandstorm: I spoke English. I spoke, and I was linguistically understood.

It was a miracle.

I was given this great weapon of survival—English—to be used years after I had received it. Who knew it would become my lifeline?

With airport security and immigration officials, I was able to share my journey, answer their questions, and explain the unbelievable world of experiences I had lived through that brought me, broken and needing, to this precise, perilous moment.

My weapon was my voice. I refused to be a helpless victim. In that very moment at that cold, chaotic airport, I made up my mind to be a survivor. I was going to overcome this and conquer. I opened my eyes to absorb the depth of the valley I was standing in.

I knew that in my future, there would be more headaches, bouts of insomnia, an overpowering sense of homesickness, insecurity, and more. But I was ready for my life to change in ways that I could not yet fathom. My heart was open.

When I think back to being at that airport and starting my new life in the West, I think of two quotes.

One is by Václav Havel, a writer and the first President of the Czech Republic, who said: "Isn't it the moment of most profound doubt that gives birth to new certainties? Perhaps hopelessness is the very soil that nourishes human hope; perhaps one could never find sense in life without first experiencing its absurdity."[9]

The other is by Albert Einstein, who said, "The important thing is not to stop questioning. Curiosity has its own reason for existence."[10]

For me, prayers and dreams often intermingle. To be

clear, when I say dreams, I do not mean life goals or career ambitions. I mean the dreams we experience while sleeping—the Technicolor and symphonic ideas, emotions, images, and feelings that we experience while asleep.

When I am in bed, just before I go to sleep, I have a quick private exchange with God. I face the Holy Spirit to have an intimate moment with him. Usually, I ask questions. If he does not provide any answers straight away, I often say something such as, *"I hope to hear from you before I fall asleep. But if I don't, would you visit me in my dreams?"*

There are no higher heights or deeper depths than where we go in prayer with God. Dare to be bold. Dare to stand on God's promises. Instead of just reading the Bible, circle his promises, transcribe them in a personal notebook, read them out loud. Remind him of his words, promises, and love. God does not forget. He is the lover of your soul. Our voices are like fingerprints and snowflakes—no two are identical. I cannot sing your hallelujah; you have to sing it.

When you pray, keep a prayer journal. A prayer journal will provide you with focus, help you to keep track of your spiritual progress, and draw you closer to God.

God wants us to pray specific prayers. Being specific clarifies our intentions. It helps us to distinguish between our wants and needs, and it increases our faith.

Miracles are not something new. They are not wishes come true. They are not New Age. They are not black magic.

Miracles do not belong to just a particular religion or a certain set of people.

Miracles are breathtaking. They are filled with color, emotions, change, and wonder.

I have had my fair share of miracles.

I have a desire to search for truth—that is a miracle.

I survived the soul-wrenching darkness of war—another miracle.

I met the Holy Spirit—the best miracle of all.

I often receive invitations from churches to join them in prayer or to lead a prayer meeting. Often these invitations concern praying for entire nations or faraway places around the world that you and I could barely even pronounce, let alone find on a map. Still, everywhere people are being led to Christ, and that is an incredible miracle.

We are regularly bombarded by news about amazing, positive, healthy things happening around the world. The culture is changing so dramatically. Why has the pace of cultural change increased? There is a divine wave of change that is reshaping the value system of people who do not even know him yet.

Jesus left everything and came down from Heaven for you, me, and everyone else. Do not think, even for a moment, that you do not matter, that you are forgotten. He knows your name, your address, your circumstances. He understands what inspires, confuses, and upsets you. He loves you beyond measure. He holds you when you are crying, collecting every tear. On nights when you are too afraid to sleep because of nightmares, he watches over you.

And yet, God is full of mystery. We cannot completely figure him out. If we could figure him out, he would not be God.

Jesus came in the form of a man. He made it clear that he was not here to abolish the law, but to fulfill the law (Matthew 5:17). Jesus experienced hunger and thirst when he was sent into the wilderness by the Holy Spirit after he was baptized by John the Baptist. He experienced emotions of anger, just like you and I, when he was at the synagogue. In the garden of Gethsemane, as he prayed and had the world on his mind, drops of blood dripped down from his forehead.

He experienced compassion towards all who were broken and ill, tormented by spirits, or accused by the law, such as the woman who was to be stoned. He got down on her level and looked into her soul with his piercing eyes that carried love and justice. He spoke grace, saying, "Let any one of you who is without sin be the first to throw a stone at her" (John 8:7).

And there was the woman who crawled beneath the feet of hundreds of people who wanted to meet Jesus and wanted his attention. Jesus felt a withdrawal from his spiritual bank account. He was one with the Father, yet he was fully aware of the demonic and dead who craved life. He was aware when faith showed up. She believed that if she could touch the hem of his robes, then she would be healed. And Jesus knew the moment that happened. He asked his disciples, "Who touched me?" (Luke 8:45). The multitudes were touching Jesus, yet she got to the hem of his holy robes. His attention shifted because of her faith, and she was healed.

Miracles do not just belong to the Old Testament and the New Testament; they happen today.

We sometimes feel spiritually alone and doubt the power of prayer. Once, when I was young, I spoke my heart to God:

"I really do not feel that I need this. I know I was born to worship you, but you do not need my worship. Besides, my worship is not good enough. I could sit here all day and be bored out of my mind praying, and it would be inadequate because it is not coming from the heart. Also, when I am praying, I am not even thinking of you. I am just going through the motions. I am not even paying attention to my words, so I can't guarantee that my prayers are being heard."

We sometimes feel stuck in our lives. But if we can just keep an eye focused on every step we take, at least we know there is forward movement. We can tell ourselves, *"I am going through this. I am not stuck. I am still moving."*

We doubt ourselves too much. *"Did I do such-and-such right? Should I have done this or that differently?"* We lose precious moments of our lives to guilt and shame. If we just stand still, we can remind ourselves that God has our backs. He is looking after us. Everything will turn out according to his plan.

Have you ever noticed that fear has the power to rob you of peace? Well, a lack of belief has a similar effect on miracles. In short, unbelief blocks you from experiencing miracles.

I have been among people who do not believe in God.

I have had close friendships with non-believers. If they could just get out of their prison of unbelief, fear, and doubt, if they could rescind their partnerships with lies, they would no longer be locked out of experiencing miracles.

Wonders and marvels are all around us, but there is something preventing people from categorizing them as miracles. Are the following miracles: the healing of a paralyzed person, storms being stilled, the birth of a baby, a friendship between two people whom society thinks should never be friends? Yes! All of them are certainly miracles.

Deep down, I know there is no simple formula that one can follow to experience the miraculous. Let me be resolute and clear about this: God is the Miracle Worker. He is the Way Maker. Salvation is by grace through faith.

What you pursue determines what you get. My quest is clear—I want more of God. What is your quest?

I would like to end this chapter with three suggestions about prayer that have always worked for me and always warmed my heart. My recommendations are to pray desperately, to pray intensely, and to pray consistently.

Pray desperately. When we pray desperately, it is often when we are praying alone. Maybe it is when you are at home, after everyone else is asleep, and you are all alone with your thoughts, feelings, and God. You cry out with a sense of desperation, *"Do you hear me? Do you see me? I am right here. Have you forgotten about me?"* These are forlorn calls. We are reaching out to the divine, so high. We are all broken in one way or another.

Pray intensely. In order to meet the miraculous, you have to go from a place of unbelief to a place of belief. Using faith, tap into the supernatural, the divine. That is where you bridge the seen and the unseen. That is where you bridge what you can touch and what's untouchable.

Our battle is not with weapons. It is with prayers, with arms wide open.

Pray consistently. What does it mean to pray consistently? Personally, I do not believe that it is necessary to pray numerous times every day. Praying according to a routine or a schedule can undermine the beauty and power of prayer. It can make it too regimented. Praying should not be forced upon you by digital reminders popping up on your phone that say something like, "Don't forget to pray!"

In a similar vein, I do not think you have to end every prayer by saying, "In Jesus' name, amen." That, too, can become monotonous.

I believe that praying consistently means being in absolute communion with God. It is about being in a constant dialogue with him, a heart-to-heart conversation.

CHAPTER EIGHT

Forgiveness

Forgiveness means different things for different people. Also, different translations can lead to different understandings of this crucial topic. One analysis found that the Greek word for *forgive* appears approximately 140 times in the New Testament. However, when translated, the English word *forgive* often appears only approximately forty times in English versions of the New Testament.[11] Thinking about that numerical discrepancy, you have to wonder whether something may be getting lost in translation. But I am here to say that you do not have to worry about the concept of forgiveness somehow being lost by Bible translators. Whichever translation of the Bible you use, you *can* find forgiveness *all throughout* Scripture.

As I read the Bible, I have found that a major prerequisite for truly forgiving someone—which is different from talking about the definition of forgiveness—is to leave something behind. For instance, you need to leave behind bitterness, anger, and resentment. It is about divorcing yourself from something that is holding you back, something that is ultimately hurting both you and others.

I often ask myself, *"What did forgiveness mean to Jesus?"* As we all know, on the cross, Jesus forgave. He said, "Father, forgive them, for they do not know what they are doing" (Luke 23:34). Examining whether someone knowingly or unknowingly hurt you is a good place to begin. Yet, we must remember that knowledge—or an absence of it—is just one side of the forgiveness coin. The other side is intent. With that in mind, it is important to uncover whether someone willingly or unwillingly hurt you. In an undeniably tangible way, whether someone intended to hurt you deeply impacts the entire forgiveness process.

I know the dark side of this because in my previous life, I knowingly and willingly wanted to get my enemies. Specifically, from when I was a child and into my early twenties, I wanted to be a freedom fighter. One person's terrorist is another person's freedom fighter. The difference between the two is purely a matter of perspective. I am not going to explore any of that here. Suffice it to say that in my past life, I would have knowingly and willingly hurt my enemies. And if I had, that would have unquestionably influenced my own claims for forgiveness.

With Jesus, I have turned my back on those views and desires. That is what we do when we repent, when we truly ask for forgiveness: we do a complete turnaround. We change course 180 degrees regarding past decisions that we now know, with hindsight and heavenly insight, were not aligned with God.

All of this is about intentionality, about your heart condition. It is impossible for you to know what you can't see, even if it is directly in front of you. All you may know is that you are hurting. Maybe your ego or your pride is adding to the fog, and you are temporarily blinded to the fact that forgiveness is a two-way street: there is forgiving yourself, and there is forgiving others. You tell yourself comforting things like: *"Of course none of this is my fault. I had nothing to do with any of this. I was just minding my own business when so-and-so hurt me."*

But there's always something deeper. If you look hard enough, you may find that you are not altogether faultless, which brings me back to the types of questions I always ask myself: *"Why did so-and-so hurt me? Is this a pattern in my life? Each time someone says those kinds of words to me, why do I allow them to penetrate my heart and hurt me? What could I do to stop this cycle?"*

I often experience forgiveness in a sequence of three steps. First, I have to make my peace with God. Second, I have to deal with it within myself. Third, I have to contend with the other person, whoever they may be.

There is often a great deal of confusion concerning the first step. People sometimes think, *"How could God forgive me for that?"* When we ask that type of question, we have lost sight of the fact that though there is sin, there is nothing bigger than God's capacity for forgiveness. In difficulty, in pain, it is not a small and easy step to forgive. It may be costly, emotional, and heartbreaking. In that state of mind, forgiving unconditionally will not be your first choice.

There are many insightful and uplifting passages concerning forgiveness that I return to regularly. For instance, in the book of Matthew, "Peter came to Jesus and asked, 'Lord, how many times shall I forgive my brother or sister who sins against me? Up to seven times?' Jesus answered, 'I tell you, not [just] seven times, but seventy-seven times'" (Matthew 18:21–22).

This tells us that our forgiveness should be without limit. By saying this, he did not mean, "Only if the offending person is Christian, then forgive them." He was not saying, "If the transgressor is Buddhist, then don't forgive them." No, that is not what Jesus said. He was talking about how forgiveness should be boundless. Forgiveness is not just for people we agree with, people we go to the same church with, people who believe in the Holy Trinity.

In these trying times, we need to understand what forgiveness is really about. What does it look like? Why should I forgive someone who has hurt me?

In the book of Luke, Jesus stated that we not only must forgive without limits; there also has to be repentance. Jesus said to his disciples, "If your brother or sister sins against you, rebuke them; and if they repent, forgive them. Even if they sin against you seven times in a day and seven times come back to you saying 'I repent,' you must forgive them" (Luke 17:3–4).

Remember that in the book of John, concerning the woman who is traditionally identified as Mary Magdalene, Jesus said, "Let any one of you who is without sin be the first to throw a stone at her" (John 8:7).

That is forgiveness extended from the Father to us.
And no one could throw the first stone!

Sometimes I wonder if there was a much longer conversation between Jesus and this woman, Mary Magdalene, who was accused. We do not know. Nonetheless, we do know that he said to her, "Then neither do I condemn you. ... Go now and leave your life of sin" (John 8:11).

That was repentance. He was effectively saying, "I forgive you. I know your heart."

Have you ever heard the adage, "peeling layers off an onion?" I sometimes use this when I give talks, I will use it metaphorically to explore my life. Of course, I am not the first to do this. Carl Sandburg, the poet and journalist, probably has the most popular quote about this topic. He once said, "Life is an onion. You peel it year by year and sometimes cry."[12]

In terms of my family and my journey to understand forgiveness, it is like I have been peeling back layers of an onion for years. It is a cliché, but it is real. Every year, I peel off another layer. Every year, God reveals another layer to my story.

When I was 14, my parents forced me to get married (as I have elaborated on in a previous chapter). I know, through the Holy Spirit, that when they did that, they had my best interests in mind. They did not do it to hurt me. They basically did what they hoped would be best for me. Based on that realization alone, I should have been able to say, "God, I forgive my parents." But I could not. Forgiveness is a process, not an event, and I had to go through it step by step.

Years later, I met up with my mother.

"Would you forgive me?" she asked.

Deep inside me, that triggered a kind of meltdown.

For as long as I could remember, I had bottled up so much pain, rage, and shame. And boy had I meticulously kept a record of all the things that my parents had done to me. During childhood when I was compiling this list, I suppose I could have called it "Things I'll Never Forgive My Parents For" or maybe "My Anger Is Justified List." My arranged marriage was right at the top of that list. Also near the top was a moment when I was young and I felt that my mother, in front of some friends, said several hurtful things against me. For decades, I kept those events all locked away inside me. With hindsight, I suppose I could have also called my list "My Bitterness List."

As an adult, having that meltdown with my mother, I realized that I was wounding her. I realized that, piece by piece, I was breaking her heart. It was as if I wanted her to hurt the way she had hurt me. Selfishly, I wanted her to feel my pain.

We know that our true living God, Yahweh, our Father, does not keep a record of our sins because Jesus took the wrath of our sins. Yet, I grew up in a place where records were kept, so I only knew how to keep records. And I had many records, a long list that justified my anger and resentment.

When my mother understood that I had carried all of that pain for all these years, she said, "Please don't read the whole list. I can't take it."

I thought, *"You don't get away that easily."*

"I'm sorry," she continued. "I don't remember half of the things you are saying."

I wanted to punch something. Angry and confused, I thought, *"Are you kidding me? On top of everything, you don't remember what you did to me? But I have this long list!"*

Forgetting—that is our human nature, that we forget. I believe it is God's mercy that we have the ability to forget pain, to forget what we have done to others, to forget what has been done to us. It is a defense mechanism that somehow enables us to wipe away some of our most harrowing memories.

"Even though I don't remember all of the things you are telling me that I did to you," she continued, "I believe you. I know I hurt you. Would you please forgive me?"

I could hear her pain in her voice. I looked into my mom's eyes, and I began to cry. I accepted her apology, and I said, "I forgive you." It was as if I was drawing a line through every item on my anger and bitterness list and then burning the paper it was written on.

This taught me that forgiveness is indeed a choice. Forgiving others for trespassing against us is a choice. We have been given free will—and what a gift it is!

God can hold his forgiveness back if we choose not to extend the same to other people.

Many of us have made statements such as: "I will never forgive that!" or "I will forgive, but I will never forget!"

When God forgives you, he forgives you "as far as the east is from the west" (Psalm 103:12). It is a promise that when he forgives, it is gone. It is as far as the east and the west, which will never meet. It is forgotten.

Accepting Jesus as my Lord and Savior has tested my boundaries of forgiveness.

My circle of friends, including my best friend, would most likely not accept me as a Christian.

If I were in the country and I revealed to my friends that I am now a Christian, they would probably report me. That is, they would tell the authorities about me, and the Islamic religious police would apprehend me. It is very likely that I would be made an example of.

In the hypothetical—yet utterly possible—situation of my friends betraying me to the government, my friends would be doing what they believed they *should* do in order to be proper Muslims.

And to be a proper Christian, I would have to forgive them, and I *would* forgive them.

But I do not live in the Middle East anymore. I am now on the other side of the world. And, in a way, I am safe. Yet, in this book, I am declaring myself to be a former Muslim. If any of my childhood friends read this and figure out who I am, they would not be able to have me arrested and executed, but they would disown me.

Being a Christian, there is a price to pay if you are leaving a previous lifestyle behind or if you are losing family, friends, or your career. But there is always the reward of gaining Christ, the Hope of Glory, and eternal salvation. As Paul said, "For to me, to live is Christ and to die is gain" (Philippians 1:21).

This is my life. There is always a chance that I might have a painful death or that I might be betrayed. But the

One I follow was betrayed. Is that not how it goes? If we want to be leaders or we want to follow in the footsteps of the great heroes of our times, we must confront these risks head-on, alert, with our hearts open.

Pride can prevent forgiveness.

When we see pride facing us, I believe that it is important to take a deep breath and recognize it instead of just automatically reacting to it and fighting it. We have to remind ourselves that it is easy for someone to become self-absorbed.

Pride is not difficult to find. Humility is the way to face it. Being humble takes practice.

If someone is complaining, then compliment them.

If someone is being toxic, then be optimistic.

If someone is playing the victim, treat them like they are a survivor, like they can overcome their issues.

Oh, and do not forget to forgive. Forgive, forgive, and forgive again!

CHAPTER NINE

Grief

I have struggled with the concept of accepting trauma and simply moving on. It is difficult for me. People often tell you something like, "It is what it is," which is not that far from bluntly saying, "Just get over it." But to me, going on with my life occasionally feels like I am intentionally trying to forget or ignore something, which makes it feel unjust and selfish.

For several years, I grieved without publicly displaying any of the chaos that was still raging inside me. I was numb. I avoided sharing any of my personal stories with anyone. I hid in the background and stayed clear of anything that would bring up the trauma. No one could ever guess my journey because I did not put it on display. I pushed it deep into my wounded soul. That was my way of "moving on."

As the years passed, I transformed into the social butterfly, the entertainer, the center of the spotlight. I would attend small dinner parties or large get-togethers, and I would make it my mission to make people around me happy. But even though I would always be dressed immaculately, and I would always be smiling, my makeup was just a mask that I could hide my pain behind.

After being silent about my own life for years, I decided that it was time to try to connect with people. At gatherings with friends, I gradually started to open up. After gaining more confidence, I even gave a few speeches at various conferences. Often what I had to say to friends or audiences was received well—sometimes not so well.

I would share difficult details about myself, and someone would say something like, "That was a great story." I would think, *"No, that is not a story. That is my life."*

I would reveal something traumatic that I have experienced, and someone would respond by saying something like, "That would make an unbelievable movie." I would think, *"No, you are unbelievable."*

I would open my heart, and some well-meaning but accidentally insensitive person would make a comment such as: "I am sorry for what has happened to you. You have been through lifetimes of experiences, agony, and turmoil. But it remains true, so you must move on." I would hurt and wish I could move on, and it was not for lack of trying. I would think, *"No I can't just easily move on like nothing ever happened."*

I was still grieving. For years, I was stuck. I could not move forward. Everything seemed like it would never end. The savagery of war. The impossibility of seeking refuge in a Western society that I had once viewed as the enemy. The pressure of surviving. The difficulties of being a mother of two young children. The family that I left behind. The friends I had lost and would probably never see again. The journey to healing was a long road, and I had no idea where it would take me.

Often when immigrants move to a new country, without even knowing it, they expect that they will not only be welcomed with open arms, but also understood and nursed back to wholeness. If you were an immigrant fleeing your past life, possibly even escaping a war-torn country, don't you think that you would also be susceptible to such wishful thinking?

The harsh reality is, however, when misplaced or disenfranchised grieving people move into a new community, the response is not always sympathetic, let alone positive or fruitful. But it goes both ways. For the immigrant, feeling at home is not always the first emotional response they feel after leaving where they were born, grew up, went to school, got married, and had a career. Some will never feel at home in their new "home," even some of those who can never go back.

The children of immigrants also have it hard. They are trapped between two different cultures. They talk in a different language at home than they do at school. They face cultural barriers that they cannot understand. They face racism and xenophobia. As these children settle into their new country, they often can only share their joy with their new friends. Their parents are not ready to move on, not ready to let go. Yet, they have a desire to heal. Sometimes when children are forced to pick between their new home and their parents' old home, there is no middle ground, no perfect choice. Whatever they choose will come with its own set of consequences.

After I arrived in North America, it certainly took me a long time to settle in. I expected my new community—my "church community"—to understand my pain. I unrealistically hoped that they would help me carry my burdens. Sometimes I think that I felt this way because the word *family* and the whole concept of family is used so prominently in church. It was as if, even though my fellow churchgoers and I were not biologically related and did not live under the same roof, we were all part of an emotionally supportive network. We were *family*. But I was different from everyone else, and I had certainly been raised differently. See, according to my background, race, and culture, there was often an unquestionable acceptance of people, but I just did not have that same experience in North American churches, even though we all referred to each other as family.

I quickly found out that being Christian does not mean the Middle Eastern version of being Christian. In Canada, in a way, it did not matter that Jesus had been a Middle Eastern man with olive skin. He was not Caucasian or beach blond. He did not have piercing blue eyes. Would we recognize him if he were to walk, unannounced, into church on a Sunday morning?

Jesus does not expect us to understand the unfathomable pain he endured on his way to the cross, let alone on it. His love endures forever. He does not come with expectations, but he comes searching for the prodigal. He loves the broken. He brings transformation of the mental, physical, and emotional sufferings of mankind.

Suffering has many faces and causes. When you are grieving, remember that every human being was born for a purpose and has their own destiny. I hope we do not miss our own specific calling due to ignorance, complacency, or misplaced priorities. We need to stay true to ourselves if we are going to get through this together.

Unprocessed grief can cause bitterness, bring out the ugly in us, and cause chronic pain or even cancer. It is not about trying to forget the past. It is about not being a prisoner to your own past. As a familiar proverb, author unknown, says, "Never be defined by your past. It was just a lesson, not a life sentence."

CHAPTER TEN

Resilience

In the 1800s, Henry Ward Beecher wrote, "Hold yourself responsible for a higher standard than anybody else expects of you. Never excuse yourself. Never pity yourself. Be a hard master to yourself, but lenient to everybody else."[13]

I grew up with that quote. To me, that quote perfectly captures the concept of resilience.

When people are confronted with death, some want to live while others want to give up.

In Sonali Deraniyagala's book *Wave: A Memoir of Life After the Tsunami*, she recounts being in Sri Lanka when the 2004 Indian Ocean earthquake and tsunami hit. It swept her and her family away. The waves carried her two miles inland. Clinging to a tree branch, the water raging around her, she kept the will to live by thinking of the possibility that her husband and children might actually still be alive.

As for me, when I was living through a war, I gave up the will to live. I wanted to die. Once, after I survived a bombing that killed many people, I thought, *"Why didn't I die?"*

I was so desperate for Heaven. Only God knew my intentions about why I wanted to die, and he gave me chance after chance to live.

I believe that my two boys saved my life. They would give me a reason to get up in the morning.

Denial, anger, bargaining, depression, and acceptance—according to a model developed by Elisabeth Kübler-Ross, these five emotions are most commonly known as the five stages of grief.[14] After studying that model, which was developed partly to understand what people experience prior to dying, I started to realize intellectually what I had experienced emotionally for years—that grief and resilience go hand in hand. Yet, these stages are not neatly experienced one after another. Instead, they are a mess of overlapping entanglement.

I recently read a quote by a former First Lady of the United States that captures this sentiment perfectly. "Grief and resilience live together," Michelle Obama wrote.[15]

I have pondered resilience a great deal in my life. Resilient people generally have three things in common.

One, they understand that there will routinely be struggle in life. More than the average person, they simply "get" that suffering is an essential and unavoidable part of every human life. Accompanying that insight, they know that adversity does not discriminate. They feel in their bones that each one of us gets our fair share—or unfair share—of hardships and misfortune.

Two, resilient people know where to focus their energy and attention. They are great at assessing their environment, evaluating what is going on, and adjusting as circumstances shift during their journey. Along the way, they work on things that they can change, just as they accept the things they cannot change.

Three, resilient people foster a positive mindset and endeavor to remember what is good in our world. They choose life over death. They choose to be engaged, not isolated. They believe that they are significant as individuals and that they are needed in this world. They know they have a purpose and a destiny that only they can achieve.

I wanted to be an active participant in my grieving process. However, I was impatient with myself. It took me years to figure out that I could harness my weak points, that I could make my weaknesses become my strengths.

I did not want to live as a victim.

I did not want to be just a survivor.

Through my journey of being vulnerable, there was a point where I could no longer stand. I raised my fist at God. "What have I done wrong?" I yelled with resentment. "Tell me!" I yelled angrily. I listened. I wanted to know what he really wanted from me.

And I received an impression in my heart: *"I just want you."*

Nobody's suffering is superior to anyone else's. All suffering, in the eyes of God, is pure and valid. And yet, our individual experiences of suffering are unique.

While studying counseling and psychology, I was in a

class called "Grief, Death, and Dying." Classes would go from 9 a.m. to 5 p.m. Now and then, I would look around the room at my fellow students, many of whom would become future psychologists, psychiatrists, or psychotherapists, and I would feel this really intense tension because my guess was that none of my classmates had ever truly been exposed to war and, therefore, could not personally relate to it. Sure, they had seen it on TV and in film. They had had umpteen conversations and read numerous news articles about it. But none of them had ever experienced it personally. Their experience of war was via academia and Hollywood. My classmates would continue completing writing assignments. They would read more textbooks. And one day, after many of them had become practitioners, they would counsel the clients on grief.

But there is something about having *lived* war that nobody can adequately learn about in a classroom or via a YouTube video.

Occasionally when I talk with people who seem to have experienced less pain than I have throughout their decades on this planet, the following feelings bubble up inside me.

For you to understand what I have been through, you would have to watch every single person you have ever loved suffer greatly. Then, one by one, you would have to lose them. You would have to experience living one heartbeat at a time, not knowing whether the next missile might hit you.

These examples are not just dark hypothetical stories. They are real life.

We have known our parents all our lives, yet we do not fully know their stories. There are so many stories about our own families that simply never get shared with us. For whatever reason, we are barred from hearing them, blocked from talking about them. I no longer expect to know everything about the people to whom I am closest. Even in writing this book, I must leave out so much of my life.

However, it is helpful to remind ourselves that even though our stories are currently incomplete, they will conclude when we arrive in Heaven. Until that time, my approach is to listen, ask questions, and learn as much as I can along the way.

"Sometimes it falls upon a generation to be great," Nelson Mandela said in 2005 while in London, giving a talk for the "Make Poverty History" campaign.[16] "You can be that great generation," he continued. "Let your greatness blossom. Of course, the task will not be easy. But not to do this would be a crime against humanity, against which I ask all humanity now to rise up."

Hope! You can rise up from adversity!

Hope is a tool that will help you positively navigate the seemingly insurmountable difficulties in your life.

You will live to tell your story.

My story is simple. I met truth, and in believing truth, I gained victory. I became an overcomer, a conqueror in Jesus: "In all these things we are more than conquerors through him who loved us" (Romans 8:37).

There are strategies that train us how to think correctly and positively. They will benefit you and others around you.

Do what you do with excellence. The way to do it is to do it with all your heart and act as if nobody is watching. When you fail—and you will occasionally fail—you will just have to try again and do it differently the next time.

CHAPTER ELEVEN

Hope

I experience hope as a human necessity in life.

But where do we get hope? In what do we place our hope? When I contemplate these big questions, I often turn to the "big thinkers."

"Hope is the dream of a waking man," Aristotle is credited as saying.[17]

Helen Keller once wrote, "...although the world is full of suffering, it is full also of the overcoming of it."[18]

The thirteenth-century theologian Saint Thomas Aquinas once wrote, "Faith has to do with things that are not seen, while hope has to do with things that are not at hand."[19]

I think of hope as being the anticipation of something desired. When we hope, we do not know the chances of what we are hoping for coming to fruition. We sometimes ponder the probabilities, but often we are completely oblivious to the odds. When that is the case, it is as if we are choosing to "hope against hope." Even when we are ignorant or defiant, we cling to a mere possibility that what we are hoping for will come true.

Optimism is the attitude of hope. Gratitude is the posture of hope. And the fruit of hope is faith. Hope is specific and focused. It brings us to belief.

Even though I have quoted well-known intellectuals above—Aristotle, Helen Keller, and Thomas Aquinas—it is the Bible that I turn to most when reflecting upon hope. In my opinion, here are some of the most moving quotes from Scripture that relate to hope:

> *And the God of all grace, who called you to his eternal glory in Christ, after you have suffered a little while, will himself restore you and make you strong, firm and steadfast.*
> *—1 Peter 5:10*

> *But those who hope in the LORD will renew their strength. They will soar on wings like eagles; they will run and not grow weary, they will walk and not be faint.*
> *—Isaiah 40:31*

> *For in this hope we were saved. But hope that is seen is no hope at all. Who hopes for what they already have? But if we hope for what we do not yet have, we wait for it patiently.*
> *—Romans 8:24–25*

When everything in life is going smoothly, perhaps even perfectly, it is not that hard to praise God. Think back to getting a job promotion. Think about an Olympian sprinting across the finish line first and winning gold. When big, bold, beautiful things happen in our lives—

whether we are buying our first home, marrying someone we love, or giving birth to a healthy baby—it is easy to praise God and give him all the glory.

But who has the fortitude to praise God when things do not go their way, when everything is against them?

What would the Olympian runner do if they placed last in the race?

What would you do if your baby died?

In the difficult seasons of our lives, God and hope are what get us through. In times of agony and darkness, when questions and confusions abound, that is when we can shine by bringing our best praise in thanksgiving, in dancing, in rejoicing.

We will never have another opportunity to worship the King of kings and the Lord of lords the way we do here on earth. Here, it is a given that we are going to experience suffering and persecution. But in Heaven, there is no pain, and there are no tears. There are no gloomy, lonely days. There is no negative thinking, and there are no health problems. There is no worry, no pride, no bullying, no hunger, no boredom, and no guilt.

God says, "Rejoice always, pray continually, give thanks in all circumstances" (1 Thessalonians 5:16–18).

It is supernatural for hope to arise. There is One who will come to replace fear with hope: Jesus. The enemy, the evil one, comes to kill, steal, and destroy. But the enemy has no legal right to take our hope, because it was purchased at the cross of Jesus Christ. Jesus is the Hope of Glory. He replaces desperate hope with unimaginable joy.

It is extremely hard to pull ourselves out of the dirty depths of hopelessness. Here are a few things that have blessedly worked for me over the years. Hopefully, the following tips will help you to refind hope in your life.

When you feel empty, afraid, and hopeless, dig deep into your soul. The antidote to anxiety is helping others, whether it is giving a smile, saying some kind words, or sharing a meal. Encourage others. Hope fuels souls.

Ask for help. Do not be too proud to admit when you need help.

When help is offered, accept it. Do not pretend you have it all under control.

Learn from those around you. Never stop learning. It shapes your character.

Be courageous. Be bold. Bolder prayers will renew your hope.

Carpe diem—seize the day. Do something new every day.

Realize that it is all a process that takes time and effort. Take one step at a time. Eventually, you will cross your own Red Sea. Moses had to take every step in faith to split the sea for the Israelites. Even though you may view something as being completely impossible, if you stick with it, one day you will look back and see how far you have progressed.

Count your blessings. Do not take anything for granted. Be grateful for living a safe life, for the kind faces around you, for the bread you have been blessed with.

Be open. Cultivating openness will renew your mind, especially if you take a different perspective and have hope for new things.

Do you ever have an ache in your chest that seems to fill your rib cage completely, and you just want to burst with anger and tears?

I do, too. Sometimes I say to God, "Is what I have given up not enough for you? Did you not receive my sacrifice? I know your grace is sufficient. I know you give me new mercies every day. I know you are not against me. But right now, in this moment, I feel alone. What is it that you are doing, God?"

And he says, "Do you trust me?"

"Yes, Lord, I do!"

At that moment, my anger bursts, and my tears flow. It can last hours or days or a season. But eventually, that pain lifts, and there is a holy hush.

There is no way to control these life-storms, as I call them. Rather, you have to learn to swim in the waves. If you cannot swim, he will hold you through the storm. Then he will teach you how to walk on water, like Jesus did with Peter, because the God we serve loves humanity. He is patient. He waits. He is kind, gentle, loving, generous. He is larger than all of our problems.

He takes us on meaningful journeys. Along the way, there is purpose in every step, every encounter, every event. Nothing is wasted. Pack light because he will provide you with everything you need for the hike. He is the best trainer, mentor, master, and teacher. You will find yourself getting stronger, climbing higher heights. You will never be lost. As a guide, he will give you a compass that will never falter.

On your journeys, there will be loss and pain. You will feel alone, perhaps even betrayed and persecuted. But with him, you have an assurance of eternity in Heaven. A certainty. A promise. In every disappointment, in every unfamiliar situation, he is with you, winning your battles, giving you victories.

He is never late. He is always on time.

He is always reachable. He is just a call away, no cell signal necessary.

All you need is a desire. Once he has your *yes*, you become his temple.

He is not controlling or manipulative. He only requires your partnership.

He is a good, good Father. You will never get an "F" from him. You cannot fail him. You simply get to retake the test until you learn the lesson you need to learn.

God is part of the building process. Think of yourself as a house and God as the builder. Some of us need our old windows replaced. Others need the master bedroom renovated. Some need the walls repainted. As for me, one day my house needed a wrecking ball. In order to survive, the foundation of my entire house had to be torn up and reinstalled, and then I had to rebuild everything—the floors, the walls, the ceiling, everything.

It is in the breaking and agony, the trembling, the midnight screams, the hissing dark shadows, the fear of risking it all—that is where hope is born.

Doubt is a gateway to fear.

Fear is a thief of faith.

Faith is a key to hope.

The enemy will use everything to come against your hope.

But hope has a name. His name is Jesus. He will create a cover for you and your destiny, "for in him we live and move and have our being" (Acts 17:28).

When you recognize Jesus in yourself and in people you meet, your perception shifts. He begins to open your eyes to a new reality, a new dawn—the Truth. And you will never be the same again. You will forever be a different person. A better version of you begins to emerge. There is a new peace in you. Joy abounds. A courage you never had now follows you like a bodyguard. That is who Jesus is: unending Hope.

CHAPTER TWELVE

Joy

Why is this chapter about joy and not happiness? For me, these two concepts are connected, yet also distinct.

Happiness is conditional and circumstantial, and it can be an emotional roller coaster.

When I was a child, happiness was my father taking me out for ice cream in the rain. It was my mother buying me new shoes. It was watching my favorite cartoons until the lights went out before the episode finished. It was making a new friend—until we had to move again.

Happiness is almost always dependent on something.

But joy? We intuitively know that joy is higher than happiness. It is affirmed, not vulnerable or threatened by weather or the news. Joy is not dependent on the outcome of a fight, on the winning of a court case, on being sentenced to life in prison.

If you believe that "to live is Christ and to die is gain" (Philippians 1:21), then you will know that joy is connected to God, his wisdom, his Son, his life. Joy is a covenant with the Trinity. The prize set before Jesus

Christ as he endured the cross was joy (Hebrews 12:2). That is why we can sing the following song (taken from 1 Corinthians 15:55–57) at the top of our lungs, smiling, knowing that we have been saved:

> Death, where is your sting?
>
> Grave, where is your victory?
>
> He's alive. He's alive.
>
> He is risen.

The moment I embraced the revelation of the cross, I was filled with joy. Nothing can steal my salvation. I am going to Heaven through Jesus, by the blood of the Lamb that took the wrath of God upon himself as my sin. That is defiant joy. It is the kind of joy that cannot be built upon layers of happiness. It does not depend on healing or reuniting with my long-lost friends or my family. It is a substance made of divine mystery that is freely given to us when we say yes to Jesus, acknowledging him as Lord and Savior.

I really love the phrase "defiant joy." To me, *defiant* means standing against the tide, against the waves of despair, disease, and difficulties. It is choosing joy in the middle of the storm when everything seems impossible.

Defiant joy is holy joy, regardless of your circumstances, a doctor's report, financial issues, a sick child, a dying parent, or the loss of a friend.

As followers of Christ, we are meant to have joy. The Father gave up his only Son so we could be filled with joy.

This is much more than just being happy or content. It is about being resilient through whatever sand life throws in our eyes. Knowing joy—joy that cannot be shaken, even in the face of sorrow—is knowing Jesus.

Defiant joy is not denial. It is not ignoring events or people around us. It is being still and knowing that he is God, that he is a good Father, no matter the predicament we are in.

When I was Muslim, I never expected to have a joyous life. I only came to expect it after I realized the cost Yahweh paid for me to be joyful. The Lord allowed me to be born into a Muslim family, whereby he trained me in tragedy and war. My reality was bombs and bullets that did not care if any of their victims were guilty or innocent. They did not care if you were a child, an elderly man, or a young woman. The experiences I have endured, what I have witnessed, the stories I have heard, and the pain carried for others are treasures I will never trade.

Joy is unlimited and unconditional in the Christian life.

Joy is immersion in the baptismal tank. It is being in prison when the doors unlock. It is being able to choose whom you marry. Joy is the union "on earth as it is in heaven" (Matthew 6:10). It is permission to access God's reservoir.

Joy was our father's open-door office policy, available regardless of time, place, or circumstance. When I was little, I would approach my father's office door on tippy-toes. There would inevitably be a light shining beneath the door. Slowly, I would pull the door handle down and be greeted by his warm smile and delighted eyes. I would instantly feel safe. That was joy. Over the years, I often asked him questions to which I did not get adequate answers. But he loved me, and it pleased his heart that I was asking unanswerable questions. That was joy.

Joy is his Holy Spirit that dwells in us. It is his promise: "I will never leave you nor forsake you" (Joshua 1:5). *That is joy.* Joy is the fruit of the Holy Spirit. It is his heart beating for us. It is being always with family, always among friends, always in community. Joy is found in relationship with the Holy Trinity.

I have been refined under pressure; I have been shaped in his holy fire—and God is not done with me yet. When I was a Muslim, I believed that my purpose, destiny, and creation were all about one thing: to worship. As a Christian, worship is the means by which I choose to live. After all, "man shall not live on bread alone" (Matthew 4:4).

Praise and joy are joined together. To give praise despite the difficult times in which we are currently living involves connecting to an unseen reality—called faith—that leads us to grace, where we are saved.

And so, "the joy of the LORD is your strength" (Nehemiah 8:10). What I understand from this scripture is that our personal strength in life is equal to our joy. I know that I can never be stronger than my joy in the Lord.

In the Bible, to rejoice is a command: "Rejoice in the Lord always. I will say it again: Rejoice!" (Philippians 4:4). And "let all who take refuge in you be glad; let them ever sing for joy. Spread your protection over them, that those who love your name may rejoice in you" (Psalm 5:11).

When my "three wise men" knocked on my apartment

door, I was overtaken by a wave of joy. Even though I cried and my hijab became my handkerchief, I was swimming in an unfamiliar feeling—divine joy.

The second wave was the wave of Love. That was the day when, thanks to an invitation I received from those three wise people, I attended church on a Sunday. That day was the first time I met the Holy Spirit. Of course, I had no idea that simply accepting their invitation would change the rest of my life. It was a defining moment I will never forget. From that day onwards, I would never be the same again.

If joy could be a person, if love could be met, it would be meeting the person of the Holy Spirit. I fell on my face and wept like I was being born again. I was like a baby coming out of my mother's womb—screaming, struggling to take my first breath, desperately searching for warmth, security, and love. Despite the blinding light, I—a newborn!—turned my face to the source and found what I needed. It was a long journey, and once I had arrived, I was exhausted, thirsty, stressed, and hungry.

In that moment of my rebirth, I felt that I stood out, dressed differently from the rest. I had to learn to sit in my Heavenly Father's presence. I was awestruck with the powerful presence of the Creator God Almighty, Adonai, the Anointed One, and the Holy Spirit encompassing me.

Many will never know that experience because a son or a daughter would expect to enter the throne room without limits, made possible only by Jesus the Messiah. That is the normal Christian life. However, for me, I had found my eternal joy. No one is worthy of this gift, yet Jesus advocates that we are, indeed, deserving, so we get to experience his lavish love.

Prayer is a conversation with God. My conversations with him—whether in my war room, my prayer closet, or somewhere else—are sacred.

That Sunday morning, when God and I found each other, when my life was changed forever, I sat outside the sanctuary, beside the entrance of the church. I sat in the parking lot, which was surrounded by enormous and gorgeous redwood trees that were decades old. There were birds everywhere. My tears washed my eyes open. I felt the overwhelming love of the Lord. I felt the dead within me coming alive. I felt the demons that had held me for decades flee. I felt the sickness in me subside.

That day was not sunny, yet whenever I picture it in my memory, all I see is sunshine.

When I was Muslim, I believed that Jesus had performed those kinds of miracles on other people. But I never believed, not even for a second, that he would perform them on me.

I knew I was unworthy. He did not have to come for me. I did not have a relationship with Jesus.

Sitting in that parking lot, saved, overflowing with joy, I was also conflicted. I had too many thoughts running through my head, all of them intellectual yet crippling, concerning two opposing theological points of reference. I could not wrap my head around Jesus being both one hundred percent God and one hundred percent man.

Also, how could the Holy Trinity be three in one? How on earth could *one plus one plus one equal one*? Shouldn't it equal three? Embarrassingly, I confess that I was never good at math, but I knew that those numbers simply did not add up. That is, until one day in my boredom, I received a response to my puzzle, my riddle, my conundrum: it was not addition; it was multiplication. Oh, the joy I discovered! The wrong answer involved adding them together. The right answer involved multiplying them, as in *one multiplied by one multiplied by one is one*. Eureka!

The next dilemma I struggled with related to Hell. If I believed in Jesus, would I be sentenced to an eternal separation from God?

Fear kills joy, and doubt kills faith, which locks us out of the supernatural realm, such as miracles. Mystery filled me with joy, and joy gave me strength. When doubt crept in, I was filled with sorrow.

That Sunday morning outside of that sanctuary, the presence of my Lord and Savior was so tangible, so powerful, that I was unable to keep standing. I had not chosen to sit on the ground; I *had* to sit down. I prayed with my hands outstretched.

But then I knew that sitting was not enough. I leaned forward, my face close to the ground, prostrate at his feet. I began washing his feet with my tears. I dried his feet with my long hair. What makes this supernatural experience even more significant is that at the time, I did not know of the story of Mary and her alabaster jar of perfume, let alone the anointing of Jesus (Luke 7:36–50). My alabaster jar would be my human shell, my life that I would be sacrificing. I simply had a different reference to it, and I was willing to make that sacrifice.

Sometimes joy can be so overwhelming that we do not

let ourselves fully experience it. We are dubious about what we hear with our own ears and what we see with our own eyes. It is the kind of joy that the enemy does not want us to have because he wants to continue lying to us. We reject the message as being too good—too joyous—to be true. When I first heard the good news of Jesus Christ, I thought, *"What? All I have to do is believe in him, and I'll get into Heaven? No, that can't be real. It is too good to be true."* How wrong I was!

Even so, I occasionally forget that God wants me to be joyous. A recent example related to a documentary film, *The Cave*.[20] It profiles Amani Ballour, a female doctor who operates a makeshift hospital in a cave during the Syrian Civil War. Every day, patients and doctors alike are forced to deal with chronic supply shortages and the possibility of a chemical attack or a bomb blowing them to smithereens. The film is about courage, resilience, and the horrors of war.

Watching it, I was bereft. I could not ignore the fact that God took me out of the Middle East and I am now living peacefully in a safe country. Even though that documentary breaks my heart, I know that God still wants me to be joyful. Not being there in the Middle East, not being able to help those courageous health professionals, in a way all affirms the joy inside me that God is there, that Jesus is walking with those who are hurting. He is in the rubble of the collapsed buildings. He is in the subterranean hospitals that help and heal people. He is in the underground churches that overflow with hope and faith.

As Christians, we are called not to let tragic situations

steal our joy because God is God. Only he can do what he can do, and we can only do our part. If we cannot reach people who are living through such unyielding pain, like those in Syria and other countries experiencing war and conflict, then we can choose to support them from where we are. We can do this by raising funds, spreading the word, and praying. That is when I go to his throne room on behalf of those who may not know him, those who have lost hope, those who question what kind of God would allow some of these catastrophes to occur.

Occasionally, for each of us, joy can be elusive. Here are some practical steps that have worked for me. I pray that these steps help you to cultivate joy in your life.

Focus on Jesus Christ. Joy is in Jesus. In all of the mayhem that is modern society, when we laser-focus on Jesus, when we cry to him and talk with him, all of the chaos of our world fades away. Galatians 5:22–23 tells us, "But the fruit of the Spirit is love, joy, peace, patience, kindness, goodness, faithfulness, gentleness, self-control; against such things there is no law" (NASB). The Apostle Paul is a great example of this. He was ridiculed, persecuted, and tortured, but he was full of joy! "I am overflowing with joy in all our affliction," he said (2 Corinthians 7:4 NASB). Remember that every conversation you have with God is prayer.

Forgive. Living in forgiveness is a journey to finding your essence. Begin with yourself and forgive those who have trespassed against you. Keep in mind, though, that this is a process. Take baby steps daily. Instead of stomping around in judgment, choose to walk in grace.

Find your voice. Express your gratitude through dance, painting, meditation, photography, or prayer. If you are a writer, for example, consider listing one thousand things for which you have been grateful over the past year. I found that going on walks with God gave me my voice back, a unique way to express my pain.

Be still. Stillness comes hand in hand with inner calm. Search for peace within quiet moments. Intentionally focus on your breathing. There is an art to breathing, so try various positions—sitting, standing, lying down—until you discover what is most calming for you. I have found that intentionally breathing in the Holy Spirit, God's very breath, is life-giving. Exhale your burdens. Let go of any problems that are stealing your joy. Allow the fresh living waters to wash away all of the toxic thoughts and emotions.

Give away whatever you lack. What do you need from others? Attention? Help? Friendship? A hot cup of tea with someone who listens to you, sees you, knows you? Whatever it is that you want from others, give that to someone else. It is a Kingdom principle: what you give freely in your time of need is a seed to your abundance.

Learn from your own story. If you pay close attention, you may catch yourself in self-defeating patterns. What lessons are they teaching you? How can you disrupt the vexing patterns that regularly show up at your doorstep?

Joy is not a secret. It is practical, but that does not mean it is easy. Stop complaining. Be kind. Be good. Choose to see the positive. Give jealousy, fear, indifference, pride—whatever it is you are wrestling with—an eviction notice. Then give that negativity a restraining order.

Follow the path to eternal joy. Do not give up! It is easy to quit. You have not come this far to quit now. Learn to unlearn the lessons that do not produce fruit and goodness in your life.

CHAPTER THIRTEEN

Transformation

Transformation does not happen when you are sitting in a classroom and you have a eureka moment. That is just knowledge. That is just your mind.

Not all transformations are epic. Too often, we expect transformations to be accompanied by banners suddenly appearing, fireworks exploding overhead, and Bollywood dancers materializing around us. No, sometimes transformations are simple and subtle. Know this, though: tiny transformations can be just as powerful as huge ones.

You cannot plan on transformation. You cannot will it into being. On my journey to the cross, I tried so many spiritual paths. I even dabbled in Hinduism and Sikhism. I was not looking to transform into a Christian, but that is where I ended up. That is the metamorphosis God had in mind for me.

You cannot predict transformation. The quietest, shyest little girl could one day become the loudest, bravest young woman you have ever experienced.

To show you how you cannot arrange for or forecast

transformation, I would like to share with you one of my first truly transformative experiences with Jesus.

On one of my family's trips out of our country, I came across a church while exploring the city on my own. Something drew me to that place of worship.

I was wearing what my culture and my family mandated. That is, I was dressed as an orthodox Muslim woman.

I walked up the hill towards the church, the gravel pathway crunching under my feet, and recalled a lesson my mother often said to me over the years: "Where your feet walk, the land bears witness. And where you cry, it is a seed."

I pulled open the heavy doors to find the church empty. There was dust everywhere, so perhaps the building was abandoned, but the Holy presence of God was evident.

Sitting in the back pew, I felt—no, *knew*—that I was not alone. I looked up at the altar and thought about what I had heard Christians say about Jesus.

"I do not believe you are who they say you are," I said aloud. With frustration, a lump in my throat, and tears, I continued, "I do not believe that you are God. I do not believe that you are the son of God. I do not believe that you know me personally—because you would have to be God to know me personally. And I do not believe that you died on my behalf—because we are all held responsible and accountable for our own deeds before the throne of God on the Day of Judgment."

And yet, I believed—as all Muslims do—that Jesus (Isa, son of Mariam) was a prophet and a messenger of Allah. So I continued, my voice echoing around the sanctuary, "But I do believe this. I believe that you were born of a virgin. You raised the dead. You cleansed lepers. You opened up blind eyes."

From my reading of the Quran, I knew Jesus as a character in a story. I knew of him on the page. However, I did not yet know the person of Jesus.

Standing in the back pew of that dusty, forsaken church and then walking little by little towards the altar, I did not yet believe that Jesus was fully man and fully God.

It was as if I was being pulled out of my former truth, but I was not yet ready to accept a new truth to which I was being drawn.

I looked up at the crucifix. I took in the expression on his face. Again, I felt his presence, hanging there on the cross. I looked him in the eyes.

I sat on the floor.

"But," I continued—and this was a big *but*—"if you are who they say you are, then you have to reveal yourself to me."

And I wept. I do not know how long I stayed there in that vacant church, weeping uncontrollably. But I do know what I left there.

Kneeling over, I purposefully lowered my face to the floor. Sobbing, I did not wipe away my tears. I let them fall onto the dust. I laid my seeds down at that church.

If it was true, I wanted my tears to bear witness that I had come here before the throne of God.

I was asking for the truth. I was searching. I was ready to follow.

Often we understand something in our heads but do not feel it in our hearts. For example, we can believe that Jesus is our God and that he is Lord. But for us to believe in the unseen, it has to take place in our hearts.

Doing heart work is the hardest. We have to invite God to perform surgery on our hearts.

For all of us, there comes a time when we realize that we not only want to change, but need to change. That is when there are certain things you are carrying in your heart that are ruining your life. It may be pornography, alcohol, or drugs. It may be guilt, greed, lust, envy, bitterness, or shame. If you have those addictions or attachments, it does not mean that Jesus loves you any less. But there comes a time, because of God's love for you, that you come to the end of yourself.

That is the perfect time to say to Jesus, "I am going to lie on this table. Please perform heart surgery on me."

What is a transformed person?

Often, but not always, a transformed person has led a difficult life. They have been left behind and left out. They have been humiliated and bullied. They have experienced loss, abuse, and violence.

Still, you cannot just investigate someone's backstory to evaluate if they are transformed. You also have to look at who they are today—how they act, what they believe, what they say. Even then, it can be tricky to tell if someone has experienced transformation. Here are a few signs that indicate that a person has been transformed:

A transformed heart trusts the journey, the process that birthed the new person.

A transformed mind thinks collectively. It thinks of others before self. The keyword is *togetherness*.

Transformed leaders are never silent about difficult issues.

In the face of uncertainty, a transformed person takes risks, even if their actions make them more vulnerable.

A transformed person does not boast.

A transformed person is a change agent, a history maker, a firecracker. They want to help people realize and fulfill their purpose and destiny.

A transformed person is stubborn. They never give up.

A transformed person is competitive, yet they are uninterested in zero-sum games. They play only for win-wins.

A transformed person is a builder. They are the mentors, the teachers, the optimists.

Do not be afraid to ask yourself the hard questions. For instance, ask yourself, *"Who am I?"*

My answer is: I am God's child. I am a daughter of the King. I am born of "all that is." I am born of "I am."

Regardless of my dreams, because I am connected to the source of all that is possible, all that is impossible for man is possible for me.

I want to fulfill the highest version of the truest, purist expression of myself in God. I want to make my Creator proud. I want to fulfill the dreams he had of me when he spoke me into existence.

You are unique. Since creation, there has not been a single other soul that resembles your essence. No two snowflakes are identical. No other human being has the same fingerprints as you do. The truth is that there is nobody like you except you. You carry an authenticity unlike anyone else's.

The tone of your voice, that is original to you. God loves hearing your voice.

What you offer the world can only be accomplished with the Holy Spirit.

In a practical sense, that means you should commit to being the best version of yourself. Prayer, conscious kindness, thanksgiving, gratefulness, compassion, mercy, gentleness, patience, meditation, and being in nature—these are but a few spiritual practices that will help you to be the best person you can possibly be. Choose a spiritual practice and become a change agent. Make this world a better place.

You need to be transformed in order to transform others. But keep in mind that you cannot force transformation on people. Only God can transform us. He breaks in for your sake; he wants to break out for the sake of the world.

About the Author

Grace is a passionate social justice advocate skilled in igniting initiatives and mobilizing individuals around a common goal. She has a strong cultural competence with the ability to educate others and build awareness and bridges across cultures, traditions and religions.

She is bold, a brave public speaker and facilitator with the ability to connect with various audiences, understand group dynamics and tailor presentations in the moment. Grace has a passion for working with individuals who have experienced trauma, pain and brokenness.

REFERENCES

Notes

1. Angelou, Maya. *And Still I Rise: A Book of Poems*. Random House Publishing Group, 1978.

2. Williamson, Marianne. *A Return to Love: Reflections on the Principles of* A Course in Miracles. Thorsons, 1992.

3. Reinke, Tony. *Newton on the Christian Life: To Live Is Christ*. Crossway, 2015.

4. Brown, Brené. Quoted in *Brené Brown: The Call to Courage*, directed by Sandra Restrepo. Netflix, 2019.

5. Ju, Anne. "Courage Is the Most Important Virtue, Says Writer and Civil Rights Activist Maya Angelou at Convocation." Cornell Chronicle. May 24, 2008. https://news.cornell.edu/stories/2008/05/courage-most-important-virtue-maya-angelou-tells-seniors.

6. Thucydides. *History of the Peloponnesian War*. Translated by Richard Crawley.

7. Pascal, B., H. Rogers, V. Cousin, and C. Louandre. *The*

Thoughts, Letters and Opuscules of Blaise Pascal. H. W. Derby, 1861, p. 334–335.

8. Simpson, A. B. *Days of Heaven on Earth: A Daily Devotional to Comfort and Inspire.* 1897. Moody Publishers, 1984, p. 20.

9. Havel, Václav. *The Art of the Impossible: Politics As Morality in Practice: Speeches and Writings, 1990–1996.* Knopf, 1997.

10. Einstein, Albert. Quoted in "Old Man's Advice to Youth: 'Never Lose a Holy Curiosity.'" *Life.* 1955. Cited in Liggy Webb, "Curiosity: The Engine of Innovation." Training Journal. April 26, 2017. https://www.trainingjournal.com/articles/opinion/curiosity-engine-innovation.

11. Mayo, Maria. "5 Myths About Forgiveness in the Bible." Huffington Post. October 16, 2011. https://www.huffpost.com/entry/five-myths-about-forgiveness-in-the-bible_b_924286.

12. Sandburg, Carl. *Remembrance Rock.* Mariner Books, 1948.

13. Beecher, Henry Ward. "Advice to a Young Man." *The Masonic Review* 74 (1891), p. 229.

14. Kübler-Ross, Elisabeth, and David Kessler. *On Grief and Grieving: Finding the Meaning of Grief Through the Five Stages of Loss.* Scribner, 2014.

15. Obama, Michelle. *Becoming.* Crown Publishing Group, 2018.

16. Mandela, Nelson. "Address by Nelson Mandela for the 'Make Poverty History' Campaign, London, United

Kingdom." Nelson Mandela Foundation, 2005. http://www.mandela.gov.za/mandela_speeches/2005/050203_poverty.htm.

17. Shepard Walsh, William. *Handy-book of Literary Curiosities.* J. B. Lippincott Company, 1893, p. 489. See also Diogenes Laërtius, *Lives of Eminent Philosophers* 5.1.18.

18. Keller, Helen. *Optimism: An Essay.* T. Y. Crowell, 1903, p. 17.

19. Aquinas, Thomas. *Saint Thomas Aquinas Collection.* Aeterna Press, 2016.

20. Fayyad, Feras. *The Cave.* National Geographic Documentary Films, 2019.

Made in the USA
Monee, IL
20 November 2021